BROADWAY TO BRAZIL

A REMARKABLE FOOTBALL JOURNEY WITH
THE CORINTHIAN-CASUALS

PHOTOGRAPHY BY STUART TREE

FOREWORD BY ROBIN HUTCHINSON

KU
PRESS

the
community
brain

Text copyright © The Community Brain

Edited and compiled by Jarek Zaba, Dominic Bliss, Tony Banks, Brent Davies, and John Forrest

First published in 2020 by Kingston University Press

A catalogue of this book is available from the British Library

ISBN 978 1 90 936251 2

Typeset in Cambria
Photographs © Stuart Tree

Editorial, Design and Production team
Klara Armstrong
Santhini Koshy
Jocelyn Pontes
Alexane Rondolat

KINGSTON UNIVERSITY PRESS
Kingston University
Penrhyn Road
Kingston-upon-Thames
KT1 2EE

Website: broadwaytobrazil.com
Twitter: @broadway2brazil
Facebook: @BroadwayToBrazil

CONTENTS

THIS BOOK IS DEDICATED TO BRIAN AND ROGER

PHILLIPS, WHOSE TIRELESS WORK HAS HELPED

TO MAKE CORINTHIAN-CASUALS FOOTBALL CLUB

WHAT IT IS TODAY. REST IN PEACE, ROGER.

AUTHORS' NOTE

This book follows the journey of a group of football fans into the world of their local football club, Corinthian-Casuals.

Along the way we experienced the thrills, spills, highs and lows of supporting your team during a promotion campaign and a European tournament, and we hope the excitement we felt comes across through the words and photography included in these pages.

Like many supporters, we also delved into the history of the club and discovered some remarkable tales connected to the Corinthian story. However, this book does not pretend, nor intend, to be an exhaustive exploration of the history of Corinthian-Casuals or the two great amateur clubs that merged to form it.

If you are inspired by what you discover in this book, you can find more information about the club at its official website, corinthian-casuals.com.

FOREWORD

It was in July 2017 that a friend asked if I had half an hour to spare, so he could tell me about local amateur football club, Corinthian-Casuals. Now, whilst I was aware of the name, I knew little else – but gladly agreed to meet and hear the story, safe in the knowledge that I was too busy to commit to anything.

We sat in Woody's Bar in Kingston-upon-Thames and John Forrest began to unpack the remarkable history of this astonishing club, who he enthusiastically volunteered for and supported in equal measure. I think barely five minutes had passed before I found myself saying, 'We're in, how can we help?'

It was clear that one thing we could do was to try to let more people know about this astonishing Tolworth-based club that had influenced football across Europe and in South America. If we could help to create more interest and increase the crowd sizes, there was a chance that this wholly amateur club could become more financially stable, while letting more people appreciate this incredible story.

Along with John, I invited three friends for a drink at The Lamb pub in Surbiton on the understanding they were doing nothing more than giving up an hour of their time for a fascinating story. I had known Tony Banks, a football reporter for Express Newspapers, for many years, going back to his days as a local journalist. Jarek Zaba had helped with many of our local community projects for a handful of years, having graduated in Journalism at Kingston University, and had a developing interest in producing podcasts. And Dominic Bliss made up the trio, bringing with him a talent for football writing that he had honed at Chelsea Football Club, and as author of the fascinating *Erbstein: The triumph and tragedy of football's forgotten pioneer*.

After giving a (probably inaccurate) brief potted history of the club and explaining our objective, there was increasing bewilderment, leaving it to John to fill out the story more comprehensively – and discussions of what we could do commenced. One of the many ideas that emerged was a podcast series, and *Broadway to Brazil* was born. This book captures both the remarkable journey we undertook with the team in the months that followed, and some of the content of the podcast series, along with a special bonus episode that covered the extraordinary story of Corinthian-Casuals' participation in a tournament in Budapest.

Much of what has happened since that first meeting with John is down to the generosity of people giving their time, energy and skills in so many ways. I am grateful and amazed by what they have done and what has been achieved – not just with this podcast, but by the wider Corinthian-Casuals community as well. And we haven't even touched on the cheesy chips.

Robin Hutchinson
The Community Brain

1 BROADWAY TO BRAZIL

July 2017. Rafael Pedroso and his family land at Heathrow Airport, having travelled from São Paulo, Brazil. Like many other London-bound holidaymakers, the Pedrosos have a full itinerary of tourist activities planned: Buckingham Palace, Madame Tussauds, a West End show.

But none of these things sit at the top of their list. There is one place and one place only for their trip to begin, and so, immediately after checking into their hotel, Rafael and his family are in a taxi shooting down the A3. Destination: Tolworth - a rather unremarkable suburb within the Royal Borough of Kingston-upon-Thames, thirteen miles south-west of central London.

On its outskirts lies a seemingly unremarkable sports ground with a capacity of two thousand and just a hundred and sixty one seats. King George's Field is hidden away down a slip road, and on the day of the Pedrosos' visit, there is no match, not even a training session. This Brazilian family, after travelling six thousand miles to London, have immediately set course for a small non-league football ground that is today sitting entirely empty. It is the home of Corinthian-Casuals FC of the Bostik League South Division in the eighth tier of English football.

Why would the inhabitants of the world's most successful footballing nation make a pilgrimage to

◀ *Brazilian supporter Rafael Gavazzi is invited to the Corinthian-Casuals dressing room after a home match*

a club in a league so low down the pyramid that you struggle to find live scores on a matchday? Why would they shun London's most spectacular landmarks for the somewhat less salubrious sights of this town on the border between Surrey and south-west London? What links Tolworth *Broadway to Brazil*?

Over the course of the 2017/18 season, the *Broadway to Brazil* podcast team unravelled this mystery and told the fascinating story of the Corinthian-Casuals. We spoke to players, supporters, coaches, historians, writers, commentators, and general eccentrics associated with the club, all while following their present day fortunes. How is it that they were once considered the game's first global superstars? What is their connection with Real Madrid? And why on earth are they so loved by the Pedroso family and many others in Brazil?

At this stage you are probably wondering why the Corinthian-Casuals – or perhaps if you're not so au fait with non league football, *who* are the Corinthian-Casuals? And was there really enough mileage in a small amateur football team to fill an entire podcast series? Well, yes, quite frankly. For the Casuals are like few other clubs on the planet. Indeed, being the first team to take the game outside of Europe, the very origins of some of the planet's other clubs can be directly traced to the history of the original Corinthian FC, who were founded 135 years prior to this series being recorded, in September 1882. They merged with Casuals FC in 1939 to create Corinthian-Casuals.

Fiercely committed to an amateur ethos since Corinthian FC's original formation, this club has made punching above its weight a trademark habit. A few facts to tease you in: Manchester United travelled down to play Corinthian in 1904, and lost 11-3, which remains United's heaviest defeat on record. Corinthian remains the only club side to have ever provided the entire starting XI for an England match. Even legendary Brazilian footballer Sócrates once took to the field in the club's shirt.

It's also our local club; as football enthusiasts, we were particularly surprised when the club's existence, and its rich illustrious history, were first brought to our attention. How had we missed the fact that just off the A3, down the road from our homes, you could find this legendary club of sporting folklore?

We weren't alone in our ignorance though, as we discovered on our first matchday trip along Tolworth Broadway, the small town's commercial centre. The first thing we did was pop into some of the businesses on the way to the ground and chat to a few locals to get a sense of their knowledge of the club. The first response we received was fairly typical:

TOLWORTH SHOP OWNER: Local football team? Never heard of them. No idea. Sorry, there's a local football team around here?

Having said that, there were a select few who were familiar with the Casuals – but less as supporters, and more through personal connections to people who had played or worked for the club.

Now contrast this apparent lack of local enthusiasm with the story of Rafael Pedroso, whose visit to King George's Field was described in our introduction. Rafael and his family are fans of Sport Club Corinthians Paulista - better known as Corinthians – from São Paulo, Brazil. At the time of recording, they were six times national champions of Brazil, once champions of South America, and two-times world champions, having won the FIFA Club World Championship in 2000 and 2012.

As you may have worked out, these global giants are so named because of the original English Corinthian FC, who toured South America in 1910 and inspired a group of railway workers to set up Brazil's first ever working class club. Rafael and his family's trip to the Corinthian-Casuals this summer was in fact a pilgrimage. And when they turned up

Juevan Spencer wheels away in delight ▶ at scoring a 94th minute winner against Grays Athletic in the FA Trophy

at what normally would've been an entirely empty ground, club committee member and volunteer John Forrest happened to be there giving the stadium a lick of paint.

JOHN FORREST: We get a lot of Brazilians coming to visit which is wonderful. Whether Corinthian Paulista fans who live in London or those on holiday, they make this pilgrimage down here and it's a wonderful thing. When the Pedrosos came it was in the middle of summer, in the middle of the week and I just happened to be up here doing some painting, having taken an afternoon off work.

I was here by myself, just painting away, enjoying the sunshine. And I noticed three people who just sort of walked in - I'd left the gates open. And sure enough they were Brazilians as well. They were absolutely lovely people and they'd really just arrived the night before; this was the first thing they wanted to do. They wanted to come down here and see the ground because they were all devout Corinthians Paulista fans, which makes them part of our great international family. Brothers in football as we say.

It does make you wonder how many people might actually show up in the week hoping there will be somebody here, and find the gates locked. The Pedrosos lucked out that day – I showed them around, they took a lot of photographs. I also happened to have the keys for the club shop. They were delighted that they were able to buy some souvenirs.

Of course we had to catch up with Rafael himself. Speaking from his home in Brazil, he explained why visiting the home of the Corinthian-Casuals was of such importance to him and his family.

RAFAEL PEDROSO: Not London, not Big Ben. The first thing was to get a taxi straight to King George's Field. That was the first place we wanted to visit because we are totally passionate about Corinthians

▼ Brazilian fans of Corinthians Paulista in attendance at the Corinthian-Casuals

Paulista in Brazil. My whole family supports Corinthians – my dad, my uncle, my mum - and I used to go to the games when I was a little boy.

We've read about Corinthian FC's history in books and on websites, but we wanted to see it and learn more about it. It was amazing how we were welcomed by John, how he explained the story and how it truly has everything to do with Corinthians Paulista. It was great to see the origin of our club, where we came from.

It was great to see that no matter the size, no matter the structure, no matter the staffing, it's the same passion. That was something that is totally the same: we're all passionate about Corinthians. No matter if it's Corinthian-Casuals, Corinthians Paulista, we are all passionate.

Rafael is not alone. Fans and staff at the Casuals are used to the sight of Brazilians posing for photos in front of the ground, whilst Brazilian flags and banners – some donated by Corinthians Paulista fans – can be seen around the pitch on matchdays.

▲ *Brazilian Paulista fans young and old flock to King George's Field throughout the season*

It's an extraordinary situation in which so many people who live in the club's vicinity have no clue as to its existence, whilst thousands of others on the other side of the Atlantic hold the club in the highest possible regard.

Meanwhile, there was a football season underway, and we soon found out that Corinthians are not just an historical fascination, but also a pretty remarkable team in the present day. Their devotion to amateurism is not an empty platitude - it is a stated commitment to never run the club for any reason other than the love of the game. In other words, no financial incentives - for players, staff, committee members, or even podcast production teams.

As manager James Bracken testified, having no budget whatsoever – at a level in which most other clubs are at least semi professional – poses some sizeable challenges. Having had an enormously successful season in 2016/17, Bracken lost nine of his players to rival clubs offering salaried contracts the following summer.

JAMES BRACKEN: *It's not difficult – it's impossible. Take any team – you take Hastings, you take Greenwich, take nine of their best players and you wouldn't tip them to do well the following season. And they've got a budget to replace them. Obviously we have to do it with no budget to replace anybody.*

I've got no problems with any of the boys that have left. I'll only judge them on what they do when they go out there in the shirt for us. They haven't gone at bad times, they've gone at the end of a season which is the right thing to do if you're going to move. So fair enough and good luck to them. But it is very very difficult to replace them.

We've just lost Shaun Okojie, who scored forty goals for us last season. Before that I'd challenged him: I wanted to keep him, so I said to him that the best thing you can do is stay here, score forty goals and get your move. And he scored forty goals – on the nose! – and got his move. I'll take my hat off to him, he's done it properly.

Just a note on that 2016/17 season: the Casuals ended it on fire, winning ten of their last eleven league games, scoring thirty-one goals in the process, to finish fourth in the table and earn a place in the play-offs. In the semi-finals of the play-offs, they beat Greenwich Borough 4-3 away from home, despite losing a man to a red card in the twentieth minute. However, after dominating the final but failing to score, Casuals were denied promotion on penalties. Club stalwart Dave Hodges, in his 300th appearance for the club, cruelly had his spot-kick saved by a goalkeeper in superhuman form, and Dorking Wanderers, instead of Corinthian-Casuals, progressed to the Bostik League Premier Division, the seventh tier of English football. One of the 967 spectators there was a São Paulo resident by the

▼ *Penalties in the 2016/17 play-off final*

name of Danilu Augusto, who had made a twelve thousand miles round trip to Dorking specifically to attend the match.

During that season, despite their ultimate disappointment, James Bracken's team played so well that some onlookers had questioned whether the club was secretly paying its players.

JB: *People were suggesting we might have a budget last year. People within our league, managers who I have respect for, started piping up with, 'there's no way they don't pay'. No, I am doing it on no budget. 'Why don't you have a go?' That's what I would say. All these people who think that they're doing well on big money. You come and run the team on nothing and just see quite how hard it is.*

There's a lot of talk about people spending a lot of money. And they're having a real go. I've heard every other manager say we're going for promotion this year. Obviously my budget hasn't changed, I've got the same as I had the last two, so my view is, why didn't you try and win it last year? What, because you've got an extra £300 a week this year? That unfortunately is the way that every manager thinks and maybe in the real world, outside of what I'm trying to do, perhaps that is how it works. Usually the team with the bigger budgets are at the top of the league and the teams with the lower budgets are at the bottom of the league, that is the way it is.

I saw the odds for winning the league this year, we're joint second. Which in some ways is absolutely scandalous. To lose nine players, have no resources to replace them, to say that we're second favourites, with all the teams that are in this league, with all the money that flies around, for me it's ludicrous.

Nonetheless, when we recorded our first episode, the Casuals were continuing to defy their lack of resources and sat in third place after eleven games. Could Bracken's boys maintain this form and go one better than the previous season? We were going to be there to find out, as part of a journey of discovery into the world of this amateur football team punching above its weight in the sprawling morass of modern football thanks to the volunteer-heroes who have ensured the Corinthian-Casuals' survival, year in, year out. And where better to start than by uncovering the club's incredible history?

Listen to the full episode here:

SCAN ME

2 CRUSH THE SHAMATEURS

When we started recording *Broadway to Brazil*, the couple of hundred hardcore fans who turned up for almost every home game were being richly rewarded. The club continued to overperform relative to its lack of budget, and in November 2017 they even rose to the very top of the Bostik South Division. But why didn't they pay their players unlike everyone else? How did it affect their performances on the field? How do they compete, today and in years gone by? To understand that, we had to delve deeper into the club's history, starting with the founding of the original Corinthian FC in 1882.

English football was a very different game in the Victorian era. This was six years before there was even a league system to speak of, and only ten years after the first ever codified international took place between England and Scotland, sparking the world's oldest football rivalry that continues to this day. In fact, England's poor early performances in this fixture lie at the very root of Corinthian football history.

One man became so frustrated by England's unsophisticated approach that he decided to do something about it. He was a football administrator called Nicholas Lane Jackson, or 'Pa' as the players knew him, because he was like a father figure to them. Pa Jackson yearned to emulate the Scotland

◀ *Corinthian-Casuals forward Gabriel Odunaike, who, like the rest of the squad, plays entirely for free*

players' familiarity with one another which he believed was at the heart of their six consecutive defeats of England in the years leading up to 1882.

He felt that the best way for the English players to develop that kind of understanding would be by playing regularly for the same club side. And so, in a small upstairs room at the London Football Association, Jackson and some of the best players in his contact book met under gaslight and agreed to form the Corinthian Football Club.

Today if you ask Google to define Corinthian for you, it will tell you that it is either an inhabitant of the ancient city of Corinth, or an adjective that means 'involving the highest standards of amateur sportsmanship'. That definition is the effect rather than the cause of the naming of Pa Jackson's enterprise. Back in the 1880s, you'd more likely hear it described as a 'gentleman of fashion and pleasure' – in other words, the type of gentleman who had enough money and social standing to devote a lot of their time to kicking a ball around without being paid for it.

Rob Cavallini is a football author who has written books on the history of Corinthian FC, Casuals FC, and the post-merger Corinthian-Casuals FC. He explained how Pa's project rendered the desired effect.

ROB CAVALLINI: In the early days the England players would basically line up in a 8-1-1 formation, and run in a straight line until they lost the ball. Scotland just passed it around them. Corinthians became the first English club to adopt a passing system and master it, and began regularly fielding five or six players in the England side. Soon they were able to start beating Scotland on a regular basis. Before 1887, the complete record read ten wins for Scotland, two for England, and four draws. A few years after the club was established, in the period between 1888 and 1895, Scotland won just once. Two were drawn and England won every other fixture.

The Corinthian-Casuals were the backbone of the side for quite a few years in this period. No other

amateur club by that stage was really contributing many players. So it was the Corinthians leading the amateur world.

Over a hundred England caps were awarded to Corinthian players in the club's first eighteen years - which is impressive when you consider that there were generally only around three international matches a year. Most tellingly, in England's 1894 and 1895 fixtures against Wales the entire starting eleven was made up of Corinthians. England by name, Corinthian by nature. They remain the only club in English football history with such a claim.

However, the game rapidly developed beyond amateurism. The Football League was founded in 1888, three years after professionalism was legalised by the FA. Until this point, many clubs had illegally circumvented FA rules by paying their players 'under the table', a concept that would become known as 'shamateurism'. The Corinthians, however, had no desire to join this league system, nor the already established FA Cup. They may have made the England side more competitive, but the club themselves had no interest in competitive football.

RC: They were amateur from the start. There were no ambitions to become professional players because most of the players would not have needed to earn money in that way. They felt that competitive football would maybe not be to their tastes. But another factor was that they shared their players with other clubs. On the Saturday they could be playing for Old Carthusians or Old Etonians who were a good standard at that point in time. And on a Wednesday they'd play for the Corinthians. So if they wanted to enter competitions, they wouldn't have been able to field their strongest team. They'd have to ask their players to decide between clubs.

I think they really just wanted to develop the game rather than get involved with the 'riff raff'.

The modern-day Corinthian-Casuals ▶
are England's highest ranked
amateur side

And so the Corinthians continued improving the nationwide standard of football while restricting their matchday appearances to exhibition games only – although it should be noted at this stage that 'friendlies' at that time were much more fiercely contested than they are today. The main point is that the Corinthians were pretty damn good. You could almost think of them as the Harlem Globetrotters of their time.

RC: They were in great demand. They went all round the country playing the top professional teams. And the professional clubs wanted to play them because it was a good standard of opposition; the Corinthians won around 50% of games against professional clubs. The other factor was that it was going to be a good attendance. The Corinthians actually got bigger attendances outside London when they were on their travels in the north of England.

▼ *Alec, Sheila and Micky Stewart enjoying a match at King George's Field*

The Corinthians may not have entered the FA Cup, but they did regularly take part in an annual showpiece fixture against its holders in the Sheriff of London Charity Shield, the precursor to today's Community Shield. In 1904 – the year of their 11-3 dismantling of Manchester United – they also dished out a 10-3 thrashing to Bury, who themselves had just won the FA Cup final by a record margin of 6-0. As we will explore in due course, the club also took the game to several countries around the world and routinely dished out thrashings to local teams, all while remaining loyal to their ethos of gentlemanly sportsmanship, which earned them a global reputation.

Competitive football may not have been part of the Corinthian spirit, but it was a different story for the club they eventually merged with, Casuals FC. While the Casuals, founded in 1883, shared the amateur way of life – and indeed a number of players – with the Corinthians, they did not have their hang ups about entering competitive league

The Broadway to Brazil *team interviews the Stewarts*

and cup-based football. Indeed, Casuals won the FA Amateur Cup in 1936.

After the two clubs merged in 1939 - a result of both clubs struggling for players and finances – the newly formed Corinthian-Casuals assumed the Casuals' place in the Isthmian League, a division for amateur clubs in the south-east. A club carrying the Corinthian name had entered into the English football league system for the first time.

Fast forward to April 1956 and the club was about to appear in the FA Amateur Cup final at the home of English football, Wembley Stadium. One member of the squad was Micky Stewart, who is now president of the club, although outside football circles he is better known for his career as an opening batsman and manager of the England cricket team. His son Alec later captained England and is the country's second-most capped test cricketer of all-time, but at King George's Field both men are revered for appearances they have made for Corinthian-Casuals at various different levels.

Combining cricket and football commitments came with its challenges – Micky explained how he missed the 1956 Amateur Cup final due to an England cricket tour in the West Indies. However, because the game ended in a draw, there was a replay to take place just as the tour was wrapping up. Micky set upon a race to try and get from Trinidad to Middlesbrough in time for the match, which was taking part in Ayresome Park.

MICKY STEWART: We left Trinidad and had to refuel at Caracas, Venezuela. There was a delay coming off the plane when we were greeted by about a dozen gentlemen with Sten guns. I'm not sure exactly what the problem was, but that was the first delay. Then there was a further fog delay when we had to refuel again in Newfoundland. By now I'd given up the thought of playing. The plane was directed up to Edinburgh, and when we came off the plane there

▲ *Martin Tyler (furthest left) with the Corinthian-Casuals*

were all these photographers at the bottom of the stairs – it had made headlines in the papers as to whether I was gonna get there in time or not!

There was an old biplane on the runway which flew me to the military airport nearest to Middlesbrough. I was shoved in a police car, rushed to the ground – and I arrived just as the referee blew his whistle to start the game! There were no substitutes so it wasn't going to be. Obviously I was disappointed – but halfway through the first half the guy who had taken my place smashed one in from outside the box and we went one up!

Unfortunately the Casuals did not hold onto the lead, and ultimately went down 4-1 to Bishop Auckland. But despite the loss, the run to the '56 Amateur Cup final is seen as one of the most impressive achievements in the club's post-merger history, which in contrast to that of the old Corinthian FC has often been defined by struggle: struggles to find a home, to attract players willing to play for free, to stay in the Isthmian League, to stay afloat.

In the modern era this is largely because of their voluntary decision to stay amateur while all those around them have formally turned semi-professional. Up until 1974 the disadvantage that the Casuals faced relative to their peers was not supposed to be one of their choosing – everyone else at their level was in theory amateur, and payments to players outside of the professional leagues was illegal. Yet, much like the leading clubs of the 1880s, many engaged in secretly paying their 'amateur' players. As Micky Stewart testifies, shamateurism was not only widespread – it was so lucrative that amateurs were often better paid than professionals, who were subjected to a wage cap.

MS: It was called senior amateur football which was hypocritical because the majority of them got backhanders and brown envelopes. It was ridiculous. You were far better off financially playing amateur football than you were playing at the highest professional levels, where there was a wage limit of around £15 a week. But they never paid at the

Corinthian-Casuals which was strictly amateur and has retained that right to the modern day.

Rob Cavallini elaborated further regarding the shamateurism era.

RC: Players realised that they could earn more having a full time job while playing for some of the leading amateur clubs, rather than going professional. I know one amateur player who played for a South London club – he told me that at the time he could have gone into any restaurant in the area and not pay the bill because the club would pick it up. He said he had a great time because he was out every night!

At this stage it's time to introduce another former Casual, who you may also be familiar with for his work elsewhere. Martin Tyler has been 'The Voice' of Sky Sports' Premier League football coverage since the early '90s, but you may not know that he can directly draw a link between his hugely successful broadcasting career and his Corinthian-Casuals playing days, which began in 1968. He explained to us how the practice of secretly paying amateur footballers was rife among the club's Isthmian League rivals.

MARTIN TYLER: We had some good players but the ones that did well immediately got hooked by other teams because it was the era of the shamateurism. I actually had one chance to do that. The opening weekend of one season in the early '70s, I played for the Casuals reserves at Wealdstone and scored twice. The next day they made me a shamateur offer, something like £10 a game but only if I was in the first team. I probably didn't believe in myself enough so I said no, and I often wonder if I'd have accepted that offer....I don't think I would have had my broadcasting career because I would have played at a better level of football. Maybe I would have done OK, maybe I wouldn't. But we'll never know.

The money wasn't always consistently at the same clubs, so it was only when the top England amateur internationals moved that you knew where the money was. I remember one international player telling me he was on £75 a week. This was around 1972 - that was a lot of money then. Everybody knew what was going on, which is why they eventually changed it.

As Tyler reached the end of his playing career, the FA got wise to the practice and finally ended the sham. In 1974, the legal distinction between 'amateur' and 'professional' players, teams, and competitions was abolished once and for all. Since then, the Corinthian-Casuals have been legally allowed to pay their players – it has been their choice ever since not to do so.

This has, predictably enough, meant that Casuals often find it hard to compete, as Brian Vandervilt, chairman for the last 15 years, explained.

BRIAN VANDERVILT: Being the highest placed purely amateur side in the country has always been a struggle. Even just staying in this league means we're punching above our weight very considerably. For most of the last 12 seasons, we've just about avoided relegation – and that's been a pretty fantastic achievement. And now with our current success, people believe we are paying boot money or expenses.

The players here categorically do not and never have received a penny. They come to training at their own expense. They come to matches at their own expense. They do not receive any benefits from this club whatsoever, with the exception of us providing coaches to away matches, which is our biggest expense. We exist on an overdraft and there's no money going to anybody within this club other than the physio, who should obviously be paid. The manager doesn't get a penny. He doesn't get any expenses, no contributions to his phone or his travel. He does it totally for free. It costs him, and indeed every player that we've got, money to play for this great club.

It's when viewed through this lens, that manager James Bracken's recent promotion chasing exploits begin to look seriously impressive, as Alec Stewart – a man who knows a thing or two about sporting achievements - testified.

ALEC STEWART: It is a unique club with its own culture: a truly amateur side in a semi professional business. And yet they're competitive. They don't just turn up, make the numbers up, get beaten and go home. They lost in the play-off final last year and they're about winning in the right way. There's still that Corinthian spirit, a culture that's instilled into the players and into the club that is very much there.

Being a player for the Corinthian-Casuals means giving up the wage you might earn elsewhere in non-league football. This naturally raises the question: why do it? Danny Bracken is one of the club's most long-standing players, and has the unusual distinction of being club captain, goalkeeper, and the manager's brother. He spoke to us about why he and some other long-serving players stick around.

DANNY BRACKEN: I've been here seven years, and in that time, I've had offers to leave and pick up £100 here and there. But here you turn up, the pitch is perfect and the people get behind you. There's never a single moan in the stand about the standard of football or what you're doing – it's always positive. And you won't get that at many clubs. Most supporters go to have a moan at the team. And that's most non league clubs - because we're paying them £50 we can have a go at them, we can abuse them. But here, everyone's supportive, everyone wants the same thing.

I'm a school teacher and I'm not paid a lot so a few hundred quid from football would help. But I'd rather play where people appreciate you. I chose a job that enables me to get to every football match. I wouldn't work in a job that held me back. I couldn't work in the City because I couldn't work late nights and miss Margate away on a Tuesday night. If I get to that point, I won't want to play anymore. I want to commit to every week, I want to play every game and I'll always do a job that can support that.

The last word on the Corinthian-Casuals and the amateur spirit goes to the chairman once more.

BV: We're a family. Our manager has them all together. They have a great family attitude. They're great friends of each other. The success helps. If we weren't winning matches and at the top, it might be a very different story. But they feel committed to the club at their own expense, and that's wonderful.

The ethos of the club is concrete. It will never be anything other than a strictly amateur side, we would never allow it. We've had people come along that have been seriously interested in buying or owning the club. But we would never allow the ownership of the club to pass outside of the members of the club. No way whatsoever. We could do it – but we won't. And we must guard against ever doing it.

We want to play the game for the love of it. For the sport of it. For the camaraderie. Once you start introducing money, it changes it. And of course, we are one of the last clubs of any consequence who still believes this. And we have always believed in it. And that's the foundation of the club from the beginning. And we should never change.

So how is it that the club is able to maintain this commitment while also outperforming many of their peers? *Broadway to Brazil* decided to use our next episode to shine a spotlight on the man who made all the club's recent success possible…

Listen to the full episode here:

3 BRACKEN TO BROADWAY

It was 8.30pm on a cold and windy January evening and *Broadway To Brazil* had been invited to the artificial pitches of King's College School in Wimbledon. Corinthian-Casuals manager, James Bracken, thanked his players after another training session of hard graft. Despite freezing conditions and no salaries on offer, twenty-two hardy first-team players, alongside around ten reserves, had made their way to this south-west London sports ground to prepare for the following weekend's fixture.

Far from going through the motions, the night's one-hour session was a high-intensity affair, offering no hint that this was a group of amateur players. No doubt the naturally competitive mentality of the players themselves played a part in this, but the session also fell at a critical point in the Casuals' 2017/18 campaign. Even if they had been inclined to slack off, the man in charge simply wouldn't let that happen.

Thus far we had focused on several elements that make Corinthian-Casuals such a fascinating club: their origins and history, their identity, and the principles that guide them today, but now we wanted to switch our attention to the recent progress on the pitch. In particular we honed in on the gaffer, James Bracken, as he aimed to mark

◀ *A supporters' flag pays tribute to Corinthian-Casuals manager James Bracken* his third season in charge with a third successive promotion push.

How did Bracken get this group of unpaid amateurs to compete with their paid peers at the business end of the season? Why are his players staying at the club for nothing, when they could be taking a pay packet elsewhere? What would it mean to Corinthian-Casuals to secure promotion in 2018?

Despite the club's recent progress, the manager wanted more: for Bracken, only being crowned champions would do. Not even second place – which would still guarantee the club promotion – would completely satisfy the ambitious Casuals coach.

JAMES BRACKEN: It won't be a great season until we go up. And even then, if we weren't champions, I'll say it was OK. You'll never hear me say second was great. I won't believe it. Let everyone else believe that.

Ambition, drive and a devotion to the highest possible standards – these qualities underpin just about everything that Bracken does. Despite the fact that when we recorded the series he was just thirty-four years old, he already had a track record to back up his ambition. In his last job as youth and reserve team manager at Sutton United, James won every trophy possible multiple times – and here at Corinthian-Casuals his budgetless wonders continued to defy all the odds.

To understand this mentality further, we should rewind the clock to the mid-90s, when a ten year old James Bracken was living every young fan's dream, on the books of his boyhood Premier League club, West Ham United. Not only that, he was absolutely tearing it up.

JB: I was the youngest player at the time that they ever took on. And I was playing a year above myself because they didn't have an age group for me. They told me I was in the top three players in the whole academy. I was a centre forward at the time, I'd score seventy, eighty goals a season. As a kid I could just score goals.

However, James had a run of bad luck in his playing career, one that would go some way towards shaping his embattled, yet determined disposition as a manager. Injuries, broken promises, and off-the-field issues combined to deny him success at West Ham, Wycombe and Woking. He explained the pitfalls of balancing his teenage years at Woking with his day job, laying patios for his dad.

JB: I was lifting up slabs while working at a swimming pool. I'd flip slabs up all day, stack them, repeat. Next morning I went to get out of bed and I couldn't sit up. I literally couldn't move. My back was in so much pain, I knew something had gone. I knew it was badly wrong. I couldn't run for eighteen months, couldn't even jog. I got a fixed vertebrae at the bottom of my spine, and ended up with an LS joint strain that I've had to manage ever since.

But I still came back to playing when I was twenty. I got offered good money to play at my local club, Redhill. Playing that low was the biggest mistake I ever made. It's what stopped me playing. I completely fell out of love with it. I played with people I honestly didn't think had a clue. People that were turning up hungover. And I was still acting like I was a professional.

Sliding down the leagues after injury wasn't just upsetting for James from the perspective of his career prospects, it also represented a betrayal of the standards he had set for himself. You can see how this deep-seated dedication to doing things properly prevails today: no matter how low the level and no matter how little the resources, at Corinthian-Casuals there was to be no question of James abandoning the standards he demands. Amateurism doesn't have to mean amateurish.

His coaching career had begun at a very young age, in parallel to his playing career.

JB: When I was ten, my dad used to run a local school football team on a Saturday, like a little soccer

Manager James ▶
Bracken in action

school. This was Dovers Green School in Reigate, just around the corner from my house. And it had a big disabled unit. I was playing at West Ham at the time and I was quite a decent player so he brought me in as a demonstrator. And by the time I was thirteen, I'd fully taken it over. So my first coaching experience was with disabled kids.

With his playing career over, Bracken found himself coaching the youth and reserve teams at Sutton United, who these days compete at the highest level of English non-league football. There, he achieved remarkable success by anybody's standards, hoovering up twenty-six league and cup trophies over a nine-year period.

JB: My second to last season at Sutton, I was managing two teams – the under-18s and the under-21s – and we won a quadruple and a treble. The quadruple winning team never lost a game all season in the league, not one out of four competitions. And because I'd won thirty trophies in nine years, someone turned to me and said, 'Yeah, but it's easy'. I turned around and said, 'If it's so easy, why is everyone not winning quadruples and trebles in the same season?' They couldn't really answer me.

I'm a far better coach and manager than I ever was a player. I'll be the first to admit that. I feel far more comfortable standing up in front of them all than I ever did sitting there as one of them.

While all this was going on at Sutton, his brother Danny was establishing himself as the number one goalkeeper at Corinthian-Casuals. So when the Casuals found themselves in need of a new manager in the summer of 2015, Danny introduced the chairman, Brian Vandervilt, to his older sibling.

James made an immediate impact in the meeting, and Brian did not need much further persuasion – Bracken's management philosophy

▼ *Instructions given ahead of the 2016/17 play-off final penalty shootout*

was making its way to King George's Field. All of a sudden, Danny was playing for his own brother.

▲ Goalkeeper Danny Bracken joins his brother in thanking fans for their support

DANNY BRACKEN: *I respect him as a manager. If he wasn't my brother I'd have the same attitude in the changing room. He's the best manager that I've ever played for. And there's no doubt about that. Yeah, there's a lot more chat than with other managers - the conversation continues on the way home in the car, when we sit down in front of the TV in the evening. But I like it. He can bounce ideas off me - I'm also captain, so I can make suggestions based on what I see on the pitch because I have a different view. Most of the time he ignores them! But to be fair his record shows that he probably knows best.*

Nonetheless, the elder Bracken's plain speaking doesn't come at the cost of optimism, as chairman Vandervilt explained.

BRIAN VANDERVILT: *He has a wonderful ability to pick the positives out of anything. And they're not foolish positives, they're genuine positives. He is a very fine coach. All of the players here tell us that they've never been coached in the way that he's coaching them. It's very professional. And they hadn't seen the like of it before. They love the way he deals with them. The way he respects them. And he improves them – they are better players for being under the management of James than I would imagine any other manager that they've come across. He is a wonderful man manager.*

When Bracken arrived at the Casuals, they were reflecting on a satisfactory season. Often used to scrapping for survival at the bottom of the table in this 24-team league, their thirteenth place finish in 2014/15 might even have represented cause for cheer. Not for the new boss.

This isn't just talk – for now at least, the days of Corinthian-Casuals being content with eighth-tier survival are behind them. Remember that the previous season was one in which the club had the desperate misfortunate to lose a penalty shootout in the play-off final. However, the campaign before that – Bracken's first – also saw promotion dreams cruelly dashed – that time by the minefield of non-league administration.

In 2015/16, the Casuals suffered a three-point deduction because the FA believed they had fielded an ineligible suspended player in a league game. Everyone at the club remains adamant that they were assured the suspension had already been served in a Surrey Senior Cup tie, but whatever the rights and wrongs, the deduction meant dropping from fifth to sixth, and missing out on the play-offs by a single point.

Dave Hodges has the unfortunate distinction of being both the man who missed the crucial penalty kick in 2016/17, and the ineligible player in 2015/16. He is nonetheless a club legend with three hundred and nineteen first team appearances, having been around long before James took over the reins, and he hailed the club's progress over recent years when we caught up with him shortly after his departure in late 2017.

DAVE HODGES: In the five years I was around before James was here, we came very close to relegation. Then James came in and immediately

◀ *A team talk is given as Bracken takes charge in a special supporters charity match*

improved the quality of the squad. He knew a lot of good young players.

If we were to finish this season by achieving what he and the club deserve to achieve – promotion to the next level – I genuinely don't think there's many bigger achievements in football. It would be so remarkable within our circumstances. It would just be quite incredible.

Hodges is not the only person you'll hear praising Bracken's ability to develop and improve his playing staff around the club. With his background in youth football and the many restrictions he faces in recruiting the players, it has become a core tenet of his management style. Presumably this is why his players will not get an easy ride on the training ground.

Player testimony was uniformly effusive when discussing James's management style.

MAX OLDHAM: He's improved every one of us. I think we can all say as a team we've improved. And the ambition – you go to certain clubs and you can pick up a bit of change here and there but they're not saying we're trying to win every week. The professional manner in which he conducts himself and runs the club is exceptional.

NATHAN DALY: James has brought an expectation of winning. There's a certain standard we all adhere to every week in terms of performance and results.

DB: He'll watch and take away information that's going to help us as a team. We have scouting reports on most of the opposition we play against. We video our games so we know exactly what we're doing right and what we're doing wrong. And then training is based around that. And we improve as players and we improve as a team.

DH: In terms of actual coaching on a training ground you will not find somebody better. He sets up professional sessions that you would expect to see at higher levels. The level of quality and training pays dividends for the club. And then the way he can talk to players about how they can improve their game. Picking up on where they need to improve but then knowing that each player is different.

For those fans who were around long before James Bracken came in, the current team and its manager are something to be very proud of. At every game – home and away – the hardcore support unfurl a banner adorned with his face.

Then there's those who have given endless hours of their own time to ensure the club's survival. People like Stuart Tree, one of the most recognisable faces down at St George's and a towering, cuddly giant, often spotted with a long-range camera in hand. At the time of recording he was the club's press officer, photographer, social media manager, and programme editor. Epitomising the culture of selfless enthusiasm that defines the volunteers of the modern day Corinthians, Stuart was flattered to discover that this devotion hadn't gone unnoticed by the first team manager.

STUART TREE: At the award's dinner at the end of last season James made an inspirational address – just everything in his speech was almost mesmerising. And then he turned around and said, 'I'd like to give a special thanks to...' And it was to me...because of the photos and everything. And I'd never had that. That took me back. It was a bit of a frog-in-the-throat moment.

At *Broadway to Brazil*, we felt it was only right for behind-the-scenes volunteers like Stuart to be given the spotlight. And so we decided to make a whole episode about them...

Listen to the full episode here:

SCAN ME

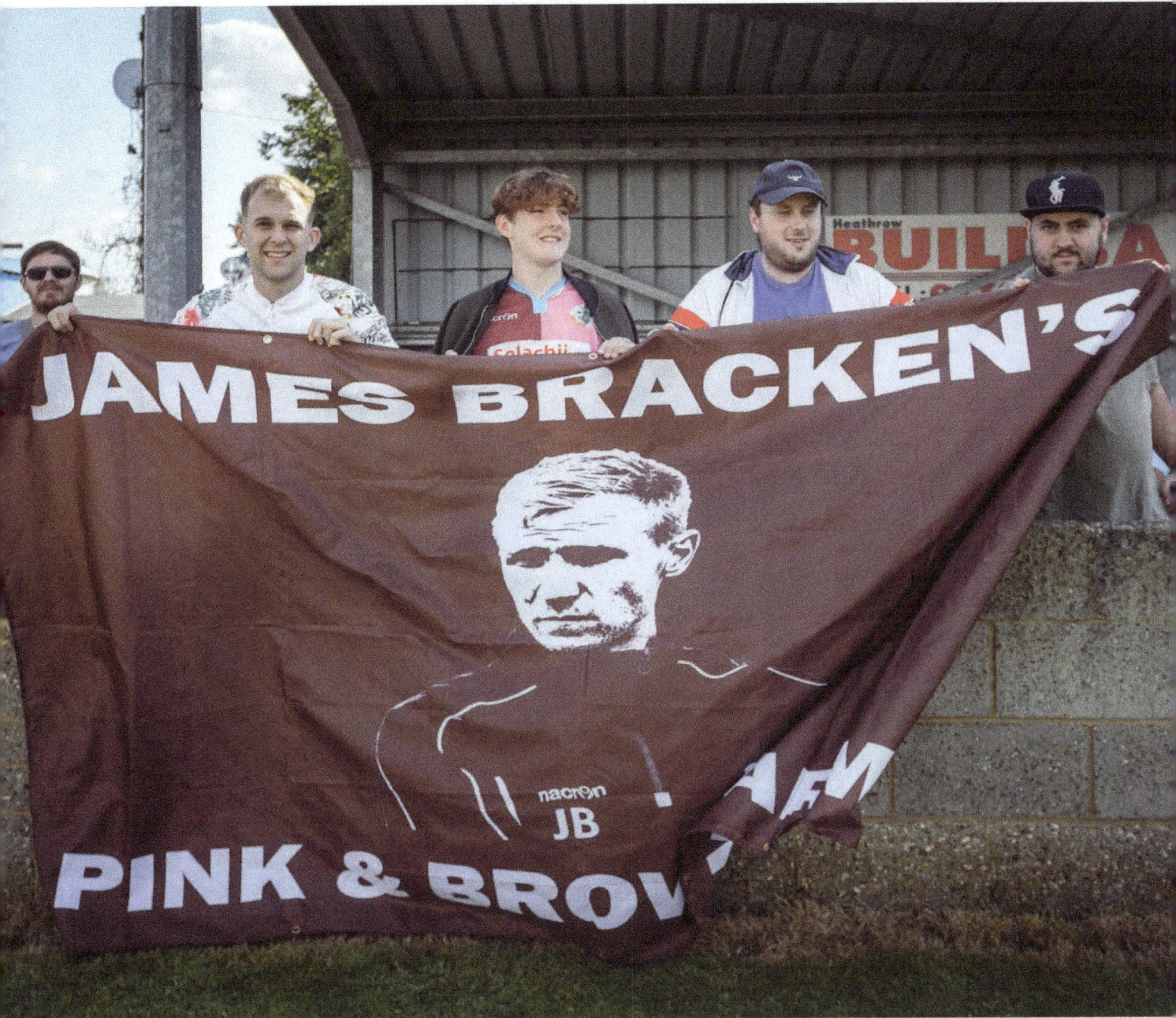

▲ *Some of James Bracken's biggest fans*

4 IT TAKES A VILLAGE

To a casual observer, the manpower required to host a football match may not be immediately obvious. Perhaps you notice the elderly gentlemen manning the gates and selling the programmes. Maybe you get to know the characters pulling your pints or serving up your pie and chips.

But you probably missed the fact that the changing rooms had to be cleaned that morning; that the groundsman was cutting the grass on multiple occasions in the week ahead; that prior to kick off, the team sheets had to be meticulously and carefully completed before being submitted to football's administrative bodies; or that it might have required an army of volunteers just to ensure that there is a ground for you to visit in the first place.

In the world of non-league football, a club's greatest legends can often be those who have never set foot on the pitch as a player. Whereas a professional club might simply want its fan base to buy tickets and merchandise, or tune in on television come matchday, the very existence of their non-league counterparts relies instead on their fans doing much more – taking on the tasks and responsibilities that the club can't afford to pay someone else to do.

So far in *Broadway to Brazil*, we had discussed the ways in which Corinthian-Casuals stood apart

◄ *King George's Field in 2017*

as a unique entity in English non-league football. Volunteerism, however, was not one of them: everyone at the club would readily acknowledge that their endeavour is replicated thousands of times, week in, week out, at countless other clubs across the country.

So what marks the Casuals apart at their level? There is the fact that the players and coaches – as unpaid uncontracted amateurs – are, essentially, volunteers themselves. There's a club history of a nomadic existence before a ground was built by unpaid labour from the bottom up. And, as our match day experiences shadowing the club's volunteers will testify, there remains a distinctly eccentric Corinthian flavour to the club's off-the-field enthusiasts.

In the eight years since John Forrest first popped along to King George's Field to watch Corinthian-Casuals, he has become one of its most devout volunteers. Beyond sorting flags, merchandise and matchday chips, John sits on the club's management committee, which is responsible for the day-to-day off-the-pitch management of the club. Even in the summer months you can often find him painting a stand or tending to a flowerbed. Ahead of a home tie against Sittingbourne in February 2019, *Broadway to Brazil* joined John at King George's Field several hours before kick off to get a sense of the matchday experience from the volunteers' perspective.

JOHN FORREST: It's very much a communal effort. As much as we all have our roles, sometimes you'll have people who can't be there. For example, Brian Adamson who is the head groundsman, among many other things, is away on holiday. So that means some of those jobs will have to be shared out between us. So you get there, you do your bit, you find out what needs doing. Whether it's sweeping the terraces or this, that and the other. And everybody chips in, it's lovely. There are about a dozen to fifteen of us on any given day. Turnstiles, programme selling, golden goal, kitchen and bar staff. The guys who'll be doing the pitch. General sweeping and cleaning up. And a couple of stewards.

I usually arrive at the ground around noon. There's a few little jobs that I have to do. I run the flags up the flagpoles. I open the club shop. I grate the cheese for the cheesy chips which is very important to our fans.

Outside of matchday, my role is largely about increasing the awareness of the club among the local community. And to show that an amateur club run by volunteers also has its role to play. We want to be supportive of the community.

To refresh your memory, this locality is Tolworth, in the royal borough of Kingston-upon-Thames, south-west London. In 2018, the club celebrated its 30th year at King George's Field, having moved in ahead of the 1988/89 season, but in the 106 years prior to that, neither Corinthian FC, Casuals FC, nor the club they merged to form had any permanent home to speak of, just ground shares and temporary accommodation dotted across numerous South London localities.

That prolonged nomadic period included stints at some glamorous places, mind you. There was The Oval in Kennington – generally known for hosting England and Surrey cricket matches, but also the venue for the first ever international football match and the first ever FA Cup final. There was also Queens Club, better known for hosting one of the most renowned tennis tournaments of the British grass-court season. For a while, Corinthian FC and Casuals FC both rocked up at the old Crystal Palace sports ground, another former cup final venue.

In later years, as the club's golden era came to an end, Corinthian-Casuals could be found in more familiarly non-league surroundings, sharing with the likes of Dulwich Hamlet, Tooting & Mitcham, or Molesey. Ultimately, though, their groundhopping became unsustainable. When the Isthmian League unveiled new rules in the mid-1980s, ground-sharing was suddenly no longer allowed. The club

*Jon Williams, one of a small army ▶
of volunteers who prepare King
George's Field every match day*

was thrown out of the entire league system and forced to enter the London Spartan League, which sits outside of the pyramid that connects dreamers like the Casuals to the glamour of the highest leagues in the land.

An embittered club, now at rock bottom, had renewed motivation to find themselves a home for the first time in their history. Their saving grace came in the form of another struggling club, Tolworth FC. Unlike Casuals, Tolworth had their own home, having taken out a lease on a ground in 1984, but the club had fallen upon hard times and, struggling to service their debt, had to shelve their ambitions for the development of King George's. Corinthian-Casuals chairman, Geoff Harvey, fostered mutual connections between the two clubs, and eventually an agreement was reached that the Casuals would absorb Tolworth FC and take over the lease.

On the day we spent shadowing the Casuals volunteers, *Broadway to Brazil* host Jarek Zaba was shown around the club's well stocked but ironically titled Megastore – it is quite literally a shed, capable of hosting no more than two. He admired the antiquated beauty of the club's Victorian era turnstiles, inherited from Chelsea Flower Show, and watched as John got to grips with the four flags that flutter atop their poles at each home game.

It can be incredibly easy to take for granted this infrastructure. Never mind flagpoles and megastores, the core structure of the ground itself would not be here at all without incredible levels of dedication from club volunteers. Encapsulating this dedication, more so than anyone else, are two brothers who are forever embedded into the heart of the Corinthian-Casuals: Brian and Roger Phillips.

Roger and Brian first became involved with the club in 1988 upon the move to Tolworth, becoming part of a team of volunteers who helped to build a ground at King George's Field that would pass muster at Isthmian League level. The project took over their lives. At times grafting six days a week, they helped shift the pitch by ten feet, erect

▼ *The early years of King George's Field*

handrails around its perimeter, lay paving stones for the walkways, and complete the construction of the clubhouse and dressing rooms, all before turning their attention to getting the stands and floodlights up. Although professional help was required for some of those projects, they explained that for them and many others it was a labour of love.

BRIAN PHILLIPS: *It was just a running track with nothing here except the building which hadn't been finished off. They'd run out of cash after building the shell of the building. But they hadn't finished off at all inside so there was a lot of work that was required to finish it off there.*

ROGER PHILLIPS: *We wanted to help because this is a strictly amateur club, and we realised that any money that's paid into this club will go towards improving the facilities. So it's not money that's disappearing into other people's pockets. So we didn't mind doing it if we could actually make an impression and make a difference to this club. All they had to pay for was*

the materials – all the work we did was for free meaning that they could improve pitches and the ground as a whole. If it's done voluntarily the club can afford to have it done.

The brothers were first introduced to the club via a friend of theirs who was volunteering as programme editor while working on the ground. Prior to being asked to lend a hand on the handrail, Brian and Roger Phillips had no connection whatsoever to the Corinthian-Casuals, but having retired from their respective roles at the Inland Revenue long beforehand, they had seemingly limitless time to devote to the project.

BP: *For a couple of months, we were living down there more or less. This was around May, April time. You get a lot of daylight, so we worked from about first light until sunset. Basically a twelve hour day.*

But then others were doing a hell of a lot of

hours as well, doing other things beyond working on the pitch or anything like that. I mean they still can be spending a lot of time here - at the moment one of the committee members is having to come down three times a week to cut the pitch. Most of the people on the committee and are doing other jobs, not just their specific functions as a committee member.

The club wasn't just good at finding good people to help out here at King George's Field. They were also resourceful in their relationships with other clubs, some of which were willing to offer up old bits of construction material from their grounds to help a team in need.

RP: We built all the stands using second hand materials. The corrugated metal used to be the fence going around Dulwich Hamlet's old Champion Hill ground. The roof of the centre section was the cladding which was around that ground. The black seats in the stand are from Plough Lane, Wimbledon's old ground. And the reds one are from Havant & Waterlooville – because after a merger they changed colours.

We can get these materials for a fraction of the price of something new. Seats, cladding and so forth would've had to be paid for, full price, if we hadn't managed to find somebody getting rid of them.

Gerry Young, initially involved with Tolworth FC and now a regular at the Casuals, vividly remembers the instrumental role Brian and Roger played in building Corinthian-Casuals' first home.

GERRY YOUNG: For whatever reason they ended up coming down here and then obviously they built the stand, they did the concrete. They did loads of work in putting the wooden fencing round. They were just motor men! They'd turn up and say, 'right, what are we gonna do?' Then they were off and they were doing it. It was just an incredible energy they had to do these things. Unbelievable really.

Current chairman Brian Vandervilt had another way of putting it.

BRIAN VANDERVILT: They're mad as March hares! Their life is Corinthian-Casuals Football Club, like nobody else. Their commitment to the club is beyond belief. To do what they do and put the passion and the desire into it – we wouldn't exist without them. They're an amazing tribute to this club and to grassroots football, in all its parts.

As a result of all of this hard work, the Phillips brothers are, unsurprisingly, part of the club's folklore. The work they put into the club is immortalised through the naming of one of the King George's stands.

JF: The two of them were the main guys behind it. They really put an awful lot of time and effort into this. We named the Phillips Brothers Stand after them in recognition of that. It wasn't just the original building, it's the continual maintenance which they do. You'll see Brian wandering around with a hammer in his hand. You'll always see them fixing something, painting something, wiring something, whatever it is. Just making sure that the place is up to scratch.

Perhaps you might think that players are entirely insulated from the type of handyman jobs that the likes of John and the Phillips brothers do for the club. But, in the summer of 1997, when Corinthian-Casuals were promoted to the Isthmian League, improvements had to be made to the ground in a very quick time period. They were actually runners-up in their division, but the champions were unable to make the step up, so Casuals quickly needed to prove they were ready to step in and take the promotion spot, but it required all hands on deck. Even the first team squad was called in to join the work effort at King George's Field, as former player Tony Blunt recalled.

TONY BLUNT: The first team and reserve squad over the summer holidays helped to build the fencing around the ground, do the painting in the drainage

▲ Brian and Roger Phillips

trench, things like that. Over three or four weekends. I've never known anything like it.

But everyone bought into it. It's unbelievable. Not many people left the club who bought into that spirit. That's the secret.

Today one important factor behind the club's recent success is the continued careful and considered maintenance of the matchday pitch that ensures a delightful playing surface for the Corinthians players. At the time of recording, this was the responsibility of Brian Adamson, who previously had won the Surrey Senior Cup as the club's first team manager back in 2011. Brian had similar memories of players chipping in over the years.

BRIAN ADAMSON: Years ago the pitch was in an absolute mess, and one weekend the first team had gone to play away. I was running the reserves at the time, and we had no game. So we dug the pitch up, lifted all the turf, put all the drains up, put it all back down. Just to try and improve it. We'd have players come in during the summer to work on the pitch. To see it you couldn't believe it – first team, reserve team players. Fantastic. You wouldn't find that anywhere else.

When you're at a club that is steeped in history like we are and you've got no money, you've got to find another way of attracting players. And when I was still the manager, I felt that one of the only ways to do that was to give them a good surface to play on. That's when I first started working on the pitch. In recent years we've won awards from the FA for having the best pitch at our level. There's no great secret - it's really just about the hours you can give to it.

Present day first team manager James Bracken was full of appreciation for the work done on the pitch by Brian and the other volunteers.

JAMES BRACKEN: The pitch was a major selling point to me individually because I wanted to play good football, and I knew that to get good players I had to offer them a good surface to play on. There's a lot of pitches that are bogs. You can't play good football on them and if we had one of those it would have been a more difficult choice for me to come here. As it is, we've got a fantastic pitch and obviously the fellas like Brian that look after it have done a great job over the years.

The likes of Brian and Roger Phillips, John Forrest, and Brian Adamson provide just a small snapshot into the extraordinary levels of day-in, day-out voluntary dedication that ensures the survival of the Corinthian-Casuals. *Broadway to Brazil* also spoke to Janine and Martin, who help to ensure the running of the kitchen and the clubhouse; Dan Harris, who divided his team between enthusiastically cheering the team on and helping Brian Adamson with the pitch; Richard Green, the stadium announcer who made a 100-mile round trip from Thamesmead to attend every game; Cameron Smith, a teenager honing a natural journalistic talent by penning match reports, and Stuart Tree, whose matchday remit included photographing the action and tweeting updates, having produced the programme the week before.

One thing on everyone's lips at the time was promotion. The season was heading towards a thrilling climax, with the Casuals still in the mix at the top of the table. Could they be heading towards the Bostik Premier Division, England's seventh tier and the highest-ever league level for the Corinthian-Casuals? *Broadway to Brazil* was there to find out...

*Listen to the full
episode here:*

SCAN ME

5 HYTHES AND LOWS

They say a week is a long time in politics. You should try ten days in non-league football. In May 2018, the Corinthian-Casuals' third campaign under manager James Bracken reached its climax. We at *Broadway to Brazil* had been there from the start – from the first pre-season friendlies in August to the final games in spring, we immersed ourselves in every facet of this fascinating club. By the season's end we were firmly embedded, but there was plenty still left undecided. Would three years of toil be rewarded with a place in the seventh tier of England's football pyramid, or would there be further heartbreak after the club's last two seasons of points deduction and penalty shootout misery?

To help place events into the context of recent history, we wanted to get to know some of the characters who supported the club through thick and thin, home and away, rain or shine. So *Broadway to Brazil* spent one afternoon in May on the road with some of the Corinthian-Casuals' most loyal followers for a crucial away match at Hythe Town. It was the final game of the regular season and the two clubs were in a straightforward stand-off for a play-off place. Although they had spent most of the season competing in the top four, Casuals' form had dipped of late and they needed a result on the final day - draw or win at Hythe and a play-off place was

◀ *Supporters mob stand-in captain Nathan Daly after late drama at Hythe Town* assured; lose and there was a strong likelihood a rival would displace them.

A group of ten boarded the carriage at Waterloo East. A set of older gents coalesced around a couple of tables at the back of the carriage, while four younger lads sat around another and chatted to the podcast. Among them were Jack Smith, a man so keen on Casuals he told us he put on episodes of *Broadway to Brazil* when going to sleep, and his friend Billy Stringer.

Billy is as obsessive over the fates and fortunes of this team as anyone, and often the first to sing his heart out from pitchside. His history with the club is absolute. He relayed how his father, Roger, used to take him to Corinthian-Casuals games long before he was old enough to comprehend his surroundings.

BILLY STRINGER: I've been going home and away since I was in a buggy, basically. Me and the old man have been going my whole lifetime, and I'm eighteen years of age now. We used to live two minutes around the corner. You could see the floodlights from my old house. When he knew there was a game on, he'd take me down in the buggy.

Broadway to Brazil had covered an illustrious history which once led to Corinthian FC being one of the biggest teams of the Victorian era, but the club's past counted for little a century later, in what can now be considered its doldrums. While the move to Tolworth was critical in securing the club's future, performances on the field at the time were often uninspiring and the team struggled to attract support beyond their immediate neighbours.

Billy and Roger recalled being the only fans supporting the team from behind the goal. It's remarkable to think that a club of such rich and proud tradition, which once played such a noble historical role in developing the game across the globe, could be reduced to such a small fanbase. As Billy grew up, his dad started drumming up interest among his friends, slowly building up a network of fans that today occupy a matchday place

behind whichever goal the Corinthian-Casuals are shooting towards.

With the club averaging a healthier matchday attendance closer to the three hundred mark, Roger Stringer has over time adopted something of an ambassadorial supporter role, selling the club to passers-by or one time visitors, and developing connections with strangely far flung places in the UK. It was Roger, for example, who helped foster a relationship with a group of Preston North End supporters who had unexpectedly found themselves at a Casuals away game, having seen their own side's fixture in the area postponed. The 'Northern Casuals' are now semi-regular visitors to King George's, often getting the first train out of Preston at the crack of dawn to make it to Tolworth in time for kick-off. Similarly there's the 'North of the Border Casuals', a fan group in Airdrie, North Lanarkshire, Scotland, who have also made the three hundred mile trip to King George's in the past.

In contrast to those lonely days in the '80s and early '90s, there is now an eminent sense of growth at the club: aided by impressive on-field performances. Week on week, each attendance seems to eclipse the last, as Billy discussed.

BS: We've seen the support grow massively over the last couple of years. For years and years it was just me and the old man. And the amount of people we've gained since – you think about the Airdrie boys from Scotland, the Preston boys. People from all over England and Scotland. It's amazing, just for a small club off the slip road of the A3.

One thing certain to result in a further spike in interest, would be the Casuals playing in the next league up, a mouth-watering prospect for Roger, Billy and the rest of the 'Behind the Goal' group. The entire promotion campaign had an air of fairytale about it.

A hardcore group of supporters, ▶
once just two people, passionately
follow the club home and away

Nerves about the crucial Hythe game were present but not overwhelming as the train rolled on, the mood being one of excessive joviality above all else. While in transit the boys made a quick call to a friend of theirs to sing him happy birthday. The recipient of their well wishes was Matt Dilger, who also happens to be the first team's video analyst. The friendly call highlighted the bond between fans and first team that makes non-league football such an appealing proposition for so many supporters.

JACK SMITH: Here at Corinthian-Casuals it's all about pride and passion for the game. They play because they love the game. Often injured players will come and watch the game with us behind the goal, talk to us a lot. It's nice. There's that connection between players and fans that makes it. The players love us a lot as well!

The appreciation is reciprocated. Jamie Byatt, a man with over three hundred and fifty appearances and a hundred and twenty goals for the club, had been around long enough to recognise the role Roger has played in expanding the supporter network.

JAMIE BYATT: I've played here for a long time. I remember when it was about two people behind the goal and that was Roger and his boy. So it's good to see loads of new people coming. Roger's made that atmosphere behind the goal with all of those supporters so a lot of credit has to go to him. And then word gets around if you're doing well, so we're getting more people through the gates. It's good.

Other players back up this appreciation. At Hythe, Danny Bracken had been restricted to the role of spectator, having suffered a broken leg in a recent match, but he and his fellow injured teammate Coskun Ekim were sat among the fans cheering the team on.

▼ *Torcida Seething at an FA Cup game, 2019*

▲ *The Torcida bring colour and flags to King George's Field*

DANNY BRACKEN: *Win or lose, they always support the team and sing throughout the ninety minutes. I always say the way the fans support the team is a major reason why I'm here at the club. We're all as one as a club. Even when players aren't involved in the squad, or they're injured, they'll still come and watch and support the lads. And I think we're all in this together. I think at some teams, if players aren't picking up their £300 and they're not involved in the first team, they wouldn't be anywhere near the ground. They'd be off doing something else. Whereas we want to be here because we enjoy each other's company and it's good to be at the club.*

As an unpaid player, if the atmosphere was negative towards the team you'd be thinking, 'Well, what am I doing?' But they're so positive towards you, even if you lose and you haven't played well.

Broadway to Brazil had arrived at Hythe's Reachfields Stadium with plenty of time to spare. The guys on the train were far from the only Corinthian-Casuals representation, a testament to the expanding nature of the fanbase. As the Behind the Goal crew made themselves at home, other supporter factions started to file in. There were the elder statesmen – gentlemen who held long-standing sporting associations with the Casuals, whether former players, coaches, or ground staff. Then there was the newest fan group; the 'Torcida Seething'. On matchdays, the Torcida could regularly be heard serenading the club's cheesy chips with a song in honour of the unique four-cheese blend.

The chairman, the manager and the matchday photographer each expressed appreciation for the cross-section of society that was now coming to support the club.

BRIAN VANDERVILT: *They bring a lovely atmosphere to it. We seem to be growing with spectators. Every home game now there are new faces and they're*

full of enthusiasm. They have scarves and they're mature adults of some age. They're caught up in it. It illustrates what a wonderfully special club we are.

JAMES BRACKEN: I love the fact that we've got different factions now, and I love the fact that they all get on and support the team in the right way. Whether it's the cheesy chips crew, singing their crazy songs, they get behind us. The boys behind the goal get behind us, and so do the older generations here that love this football club. I'm just overjoyed at this success that we've brought them in the last three years.

STUART TREE: What's great is when different groups of fans start singing, and you've got this reverberation of noise coming from different parts of the ground. We played Lewes who brought a good vocal contingent as well, and we had three sides of the ground that were singing at different times. I walked onto the pitch at full time and there was so much chanting and cheering and clapping and applause, it felt surreal. Before, it would normally be polite applause. Now it sounds like a real football match.

Speaking of real football matches, it's time for some matchday reporting. Although the truth is that for eighty minutes or so, the Hythe match can largely be glossed over. Chances were at a premium, and despite the fact that Hythe needed a goal themselves, the whole affair seemed to be defined by a fear of conceding. Unfortunately, with ten minutes to go, the Casuals did just that.

JBr: When they scored the goal it was almost a shock to me. I couldn't see them scoring. I thought we had it so right, I thought everyone was bang on. They had four shots in the game, none from inside our box, and our keeper made two saves. So that tells you a story of the game.

◀ *Scenes of celebration at Hythe as Casuals secure their place in the 2017/18 play-offs*

At 1-0 down, the Casuals sat in seventh, one place outside the play-offs. As seven minutes stoppage time was announced, the Casuals season was fizzling out in the most disappointing of manners.

And then...a free-kick was launched from deep and interim captain Nathan Daly got his head to the ball. Seemingly out of nowhere striker Harry Ottaway found himself five yards from an open goal with the ball floating towards him.

HARRY OTTAWAY: Nathan obviously got it back across the goal. I didn't know too much about it to tell you the truth. I just headed it in the direction that I wanted to get it in. At first I thought I'd hit the side netting, then I heard everyone roar, and I looked over at the linesman and I wasn't off. I just thought, 'Wow!'

JBr: That's the biggest change of emotion I've had during a game. That's the first time I've not been in control of my reaction or my emotion after the game. It all came out, it was a roar. I could have been everywhere, I didn't care. I don't know what I did!

It was a stunning moment, the precise reason why we love the game - an outpouring of pure jubilation among players, staff and close to a hundred away fans, from those behind the goal to the Torcida who had set up camp at its nearest corner. Ottaway's goal meant that Casuals had scraped into fifth position by the skin of their teeth.

The Casuals marched on to the play-off semi-final, which was to be played away at Greenwich Borough: an exact repeat of the precise same fixture last season. We had already heard that last year's 4-3 victory, in which Casuals played a majority of the game with ten men, was one of the most thrilling games of football you're ever likely to see. 'The nights that you live for in football', Jack Smith had told us.

But as it turned out, this year's Greenwich trip was significantly less tense or dramatic, for all the right reasons. As the Torcida Seething and the fans behind the goal merged to form one large away crowd, the Casuals cruised to a thoroughly emphatic and professional 3-0 victory. Manager James Bracken reflected on a remarkably comfortable route to the final, but revealed that he was far from happy at 2-0 up.

JBr: They got a right rollocking at half-time today, probably the biggest rollocking they've had all season. I took the paper off the walls. Just because we go 2-0 up, all of a sudden we're thinking about the third goal and we're not thinking about our defensive responsibilities or the way we press or the intensity we needed to show. So we spelt out what needed to be done, and they did that and they were fantastic at doing it.

There's no delirium. From our point of view it's job done. The next one is the most important one.

The next one of course was the play-off final, as the Casuals aimed to make up for the penalty shootout

▼ *Corinthian-Casuals vs Walton Casuals in the 2018 Bostik South play-off final*

heartbreak of the year before. This time King George's Field would have the privilege of hosting the final, with Walton Casuals the visitors.

On the day of the match, club secretary Hanna Newton explained some of the practical challenges of hosting a cup final with only three days' notice, with the club expecting an attendance of over a thousand - roughly four times the usual home crowd.

HANNA NEWTON: It entails a vast amount of paperwork and a huge amount of organisation. Luckily we've got great volunteers at this club and it's a proper family club – we've roped just about everybody in, and everybody's been amazing! Anybody who can help has helped.

There's extra legalities to consider. We're looking at the wellbeing of well over a thousand people instead of our normal two or three hundred. That means more food, more drink, more toilets, and most things are booked up by the time you know about these games, as this is a big weekend for events.

We've just pulled out all the stops and got extra of absolutely everything.

▲ *Walton celebrate their penalty shootout victory*

Pleasingly, on the day itself, all the newly invited food traders were up and running. A cask of locally produced craft ale had been generously donated to the clubhouse by The Lamb pub in Surbiton, and portaloos in all four corners of the ground were operational and functional. The expected thousand people arrived, the regular numbers boosted by a combination of curious locals, non league aficionados, and a sizeable contingent of Walton Casuals supporters. Come three in the afternoon, we were ready to turn our attention to the match itself.

Once again, there wasn't a huge amount to say about the action on the pitch, or at least not what happened over ninety minutes of regular time and thirty of extra time. There was a cruelly disallowed second-half goal and an agonisingly close extra-time miss from Ottaway, but otherwise the game was goalless and largely eventless. Both Casuals equipped themselves well, with the match generally dictated by a low tempo - a natural consequence of an oppressively hot day.

The referee's whistle signalled the play-off would go to a penalty shootout, just like the previous year. However, with a large element of fans drinking in the sun all day, the alcohol fuelled atmosphere regrettably turned unsavoury as a behind-the-goal disturbance during the shootout led to a significant delay, only ended by the arrival of the police. When the sides returned it was the Corinthian-Casuals players who seemed most affected by what had happened, judging from the quality of their penalty kicks. Gabriel Odunaike and Frazer Walker missed, while the Walton players were flawless, running out 4-2 winners.

Walton were promoted. The Corinthian-Casuals were, for the third season running under James

Bracken, cruelly denied promotion to the Bostik Premier League.

JBr: It was the first time I've ever sat in the changing room after a game, when everyone had gone home, for twenty minutes with my head in my hands. I can't even tell you what I was thinking. I can't tell you what emotion I was feeling. I don't know, but I sat there and I looked at the time and thought I've been sitting here for twenty minutes. I better scoot off because I can't spend my life here.

There was to be no promotion. No end of season party. The Corinthian-Casuals were staying in the Bostik South. Or were they?

Within forty-eight hours of the Walton heart-break, *Broadway To Brazil* was unusually spending a Bank Holiday Monday travelling towards a leafy village in Hampshire for the Southern League Tier Two play-off final. In a surreal turn of events, this match meant that the Corinthian-Casuals could achieve promotion after all. Confused? So were we. Here's the official explanation...

Due to the resignation of Thurrock United from the Bostik Premier League, an extra place had been made available in the league system. A decision was made to award an extra promotion spot to the losing play-off finalist who had the highest Points Per Game average – or 'PPG' – over the course of the season. Going into the various finals, Corinthian-Casuals had a lower PPG than Haringey United and Hartley Wintney – meaning that Casuals needed those two sides to win their respective finals. The day after the Walton penalty shootout defeat, Haringey United did the job required and defeated Canvey Island 3-1, ensuring that it all came down to Hartley Wintney vs. Cambridge City.

If that didn't make much sense, don't worry – you're far from alone. The point was that if little-known Hartley Wintney could win their play-off match, Corinthian-Casuals would be promoted as the best-performing, highest-ranked losing play-off finalists. Not the manner that people at the club had dreamed about, but after the Walton heartbreak they would definitely take it.

And so it was that which made *Broadway to Brazil*'s Jarek Zaba join club official John Forrest for the one-hour drive to Hampshire, confusing local supporters by wearing Corinthian-Casuals scarves at a game that featured two completely different teams.

JOHN FORREST: I've never quite been in a situation like this. I think all of us as football fans have at times cheered for a team we have no affiliation with because they are playing a rival for promotion or relegation. But I'm not sure that a situation like this has quite happened before. We'll make the most of it. It's a lovely day and there's an outside chance of getting promoted. And if not, we're no worse off than we were on Saturday afternoon.

We watched in hope rather than expectation. Cambridge City had dished out resounding beatings to Hartley Wintney on two separate occasions during the regular season and were strong favourites for the match. Hartley Wintney were, in fact, aiming for a second successive promotion. Just like the Casuals, they were punching well above their weight.

Pleasingly, the home team took the lead just before half-time, and a nerve-wracking second half followed as Cambridge City laid siege to the Hartley Wintney goal for the rest of the match. Yet Hartley Wintney held out. Against all odds, the Hampshire club were promoted...and so were the Corinthian-Casuals!

JBr: Obviously I got the message at full time: 'Hartley won 1-0', and you think, 'We've done it'. But I didn't feel a lot. I just felt more clear in my thinking moving forward. Maybe a touch of relief, but not a lot. It was a lot to take in. With it not being one of our own games, I don't know how you're supposed to feel.

Despite the play-off final loss, the ▶ players were still able to celebrate a promotion

◄ *Club record appearance holder*
Jamie Byatt, who retired at the end
of the 2017/18 campaign

I've never experienced so many emotions over a weekend. I never envisaged that I'd get promoted with my feet up having a barbecue with a beer in my hand, drowning my sorrows. It's a crazy world we live in.

The impossible dream was realised, one way or another. The achievements of these amateurs had flown in the face of conventional wisdom. Wage bills and salaries were not the critical factor in this team's performance. Commitment, organisation, high standards of coaching, and team spirit had won.

Broadway to Brazil caught up with James one final time at the end of season awards reception.

JBr: How am I feeling? I'm feeling sane, 'cos I was feeling insane there for a fair few days!

87.3 points as an average over the last three years tells me that we deserve this. After the effort that some of these boys have put in, with myself and my staff over three years, this is just desserts. Ultimately, the points we've accumulated across the season have been enough for us to make sure. We didn't get a hand out. We deserve it. It's a fresh new challenge, it's fantastic. Everyone's obviously buzzing, and we're excited to see what we can do.

This is about people, and when you see the reactions of people and the joy you can bring to them on a Saturday afternoon, that's worth more to me than any money. It doesn't matter what level you go to, if you strip it all back and say, what is football about? It's about fans. It's about enjoyment. It's about that jubilation when you score a goal. That's football, and the money is just a byproduct of everything else. If we can brighten the lives of our fans and give them a little bit of enjoyment by getting results, then that's fantastic.

The awards party was open to everyone, the club wishing to recognise the contributions of supporters as much as the players. Jack Smith, Roger Stringer and others were in attendance as they witnessed a passionate farewell from Jamie Byatt. The club's all time appearance holder had decided to leave his record tally at three hundred and fifty-five, and having scored in every season for the first team since arriving at the club, he had marked his last appearance with the final goal in a 5-0 victory against Guernsey. In his last reserve-team appearance, Jamie scored from the penalty spot to deliver the winning goal in the cup final.

With the podcast having picked the best possible season to cover, *Broadway to Brazil* had just one more story to tell. We needed to draw the link between these present day overachieving amateurs and a globally renowned club of over ten million supporters. We had to finally explore the connection between Tolworth Broadway and Brazil...

Listen to the full episode here:

SCAN ME

6 BIG IN BRAZIL

It's fair to say that the Brazilian Corinthians are in a slightly different league to the boys in Tolworth, and not just because of their geographical separation. Twice world champions, the São Paulo club boasts a fanbase of millions, with matches played in a forty thousand seater stadium. At King George's Field, meanwhile, attendances sometimes barely break the two hundred mark. Yet the bond between Brazil's most decorated club and England's highest-ranked amateurs is remarkably strong, and perhaps unlike anything else in football.

Before we explore the Brazilian connection, let's turn the clock a little further back to the very first overseas Corinthian tour...to South Africa. The year was 1897 and European powers were vying for territory and resources in newly discovered lands to their immediate south, a political episode that would come to be widely known as the Scramble for Africa.

The African continent's southern tip at this stage was mostly claimed by Britain, but British desires to unite their disparate colonies into one South African entity led them into direct conflict with Dutch speaking settlers in the region, known as the Boers. Believe it or not, Corinthian FC had their own small part to play in this tense geopolitical climate.

First ever senior match between Corinthians Paulista and Corinthian-Casuals, at Arena Corinthians, São Paulo, 25 January 2015

Rob Cavallini, author of *Play Up Corinth: A History of Corinthian FC*, highlighted how the Second Boer War – 1899 to 1902 – was sandwiched between two Corinthian tours of the region.

ROB CAVALLINI: They went in 1897, they went in 1903, and right in the middle they had the Boer War which was particularly brutal – it's where the British invented the concentration camp. There were thousands of needless deaths. The Corinthians went into that environment and came away with a lot of credit, and probably built a few bridges.

They played all over. They played about twenty games all around the country, including in the Orange Free State which was one of the Boer main areas. They were true ambassadors.

While it's true that football can regrettably turn people against one another, there is enough evidence over history to suggest that the sport can also be applied as a force for reconciliation and understanding. Here we have perhaps one of the most enduring examples: seventeen years prior to British and German troops having a Christmas kickabout on no man's land during the First World War, Corinthian FC were entering territory hostile to the UK government, and came away having made the locals smile.

South Africa was just the start. From there, they continued to travel, albeit a little closer to home at first.

RC: I don't think there's a country in Europe the club hasn't visited. They've spent a lot of time in Germany. Austria, Bohemia – Czech Republic as it is now. In places like Scandinavia there were no national cup competitions, so the Corinthians actually took a cup with them and gave it to their hosts. 'This is a present for you, we'd like you to start your own football competition'. So, despite abstaining from the FA Cup, they were encouraging the development of competition in other countries.

That trophy was the Corinthian Bowl, which has its origins in a Corinthian tour of Sweden in 1904. Four years later, following a tour to Budapest, the Corinthian Cup was donated and became an important part of the Hungarian football calendar. More than just charity fundraisers, the idea of these trophies was to sow the seeds of annual competition that would vastly improve footballing standards throughout Europe. Within two years, the Swedish FA was formed and the Corinthians Bowl remained the most prestigious tournament in the country for several years, while in Hungary the Corinthian Cup continued until 1945.

While these European trips made a lasting impact, the most seismic overseas journey of the Corinthians was the transatlantic one made in 1910.

Charles Miller is widely considered to be the father of Brazilian football, and it was he who first invited the Corinthians to South America. At this time, the game in Brazil largely remained the preserve of Miller and his ilk - well-heeled Europeans, with little inclination to involve local Brazilians. The Corinthians tour changed all this, as their skills greatly inspired a group of railway workers who wanted to replicate what they had seen, right down to the name.

There's something of an irony to all of this - the old Corinthian FC may have had many virtuous qualities, but a connection to the working class man on the street was probably not one of them. As a group of assorted Etonians and other public schoolboys – including England cricket captains, Wimbledon champions, and record-breaking athletes – they were once known as the 'most exclusive gentlemen's club in England', with a fifty man cap on membership. But their status as

In 2019 the 'Vai Tolworth! Brazilian Festival' ▶
took place at King George's Field to celebrate the club's historic links with Brazil

gentlemen of leisure did not preclude them from inspiring men of graft.

Chris Watney is a former Corinthian-Casuals player, and produced the *Brothers In Football* TV documentary that told the incredible story of the club's Brazilian link.

CHRIS WATNEY: They inspired five locals to create the first team in Brazil that wasn't simply for the high classes. There's a lot made of how the Corinthians were these elitist public schoolboys and were a bit silver spoon, but actually in other countries they expanded football's horizons so that everyone could play the game. In Brazil, it was very much an elitist sport until the Corinthians came along.

Yet, if you consider elitism from a purely sporting perspective, then the roles of the two clubs are now entirely reversed: one a non-league side with a few hundred fans, the other multiple world champions with more than twenty million. This bizarre juxtaposition between global giant and footballing pauper is what often makes matchdays at the Casuals such a unique affair. It is more common than not to see Brazilian Corinthians fans in attendance at King George's.

The history of the Corinthians in Brazil didn't stop in 1910. They made another voyage in 1913 – although without playing their local namesakes – and crossed the Atlantic once again a year later. However, this 1914 South American trip turned out to be 'the tour that wasn't'. Whilst the team was at sea, Britain declared war on Germany, and Corinthians history changed forever. Several of the players were reservists in the army and, immediately upon landing, set course for their return to Europe so they could join the war effort. It was a tragic milestone in the club's story - few football clubs lost as many

▼ *The Corinthian-Casuals tour Brazil in 1988, the club's first visit since Corinthian FC's 1914 tour was disrupted by the First World War*

▲ *Corinthians Paulista and Brazil football legend Sócrates wears the chocolate and pink*

players as the Corinthians in the devastation of the First World War.

The original Corinthian FC were never to return to Brazil, and it wasn't until 1988 that the post-merger Corinthian-Casuals made their way to São Paulo. The formerly nomadic club wanted to celebrate the move into their new Tolworth home, and decided it was high time they returned to Brazil, and finally play a match at the home of the very club their footballing forefathers had inspired.

Corinthians were by this stage one of the biggest clubs in Brazil, while Corinthian-Casuals toiled in the regional amateur ranks of the Spartan League. So just imagine how it felt for the English amateurs as they walked out of the tunnel at the cavernous concrete bowl that is the Estádio do Pacaembu, flanked by a hysterical hullaballoo of dignitaries, mascots, flags, banners and brass band members, met by the roar of thousands of local fans chanting in unison: "CO-RIN-THIANS!"

Their opponents that day were a Corinthians XI, made up largely of veteran ex-pros. Even one of the game's all-time greats, 1970 World Cup winner Rivellino, came out of retirement especially to take part. In the latter stages of the game the legendary Sócrates, one of the biggest names in Brazilian football, swapped the white of Corinthians Paulista for the pink and brown of their English namesakes, pulling on the number eight jersey he had made famous. It was a hugely symbolic gesture that reinforced the bond between these two historic clubs. When we talk about the Corinthian-Casuals being no ordinary non-league football team, these are the moments we have in mind.

The club rediscovered its taste for travel and the old touring days of the Corinthians enjoyed a mini-revival. In May 1992, they visited Japan before returning to Brazil once again in 2001, touching down to a heroes' welcome in São Paulo. Former

FOOTBALL SECTION

1888 | 1988

CORINTHIAN

CASUALS FOOTBALL CLUB
LONDON

BRAZIL
TOUR
1988

players Tony Blunt and Simon Shergold relived their moment of celebrity.

TONY BLUNT: We were told to wear a suit and tie, so we were getting changed as the plane landed! And as we pushed our trolley through the arrival entrance of São Paulo airport, the thing opened, and there were television cameras and fans with scarves. You were looking around thinking, 'Well, who are these people here to see?' Then you realise people have turned up to come and see us, and you're getting interviewed. That's when you really started to realise that this is a really big deal.

SIMON SHERGOLD: We were invited to a Corinthians Paulista state championship match – ninety thousand people, and the stadium didn't stop shaking for ninety minutes. We were invited to the consulate in São Paulo. We went to Rio for the day which was great – got absolutely hammered at beach football by local eight-year-olds! That was all just part of the fun really. Wonderful.

From the beach to the pitch as Tony and Simon had to contend with two Corinthian Paulista sides on the opposite ends of the scale of age, in baking Brazilian heat.

TB: The first team played against the Corinthians Under-21s in front of around three thousand fans – it was crazy, their fans are incredible. I was playing at right-back and I was yelling at the midfield, 'Get tight, get tight!' because they were killing us. I remember a teammate turning around and saying, 'You haven't been in the sun yet, have you?' The stand was so big, my area was covered in shade, and as soon as I moved into the sun I realised how hot it was! We lost 2-0 but it was a good game.

The veterans were up next, but most of our vets had got injured, having played three games on the tour already. Because Simon and I were a bit older,

we had to play in the vets match straight after! To play for the Corinthians vets you had to have won the Brazilian league, so they've got internationals, the lot. They had three or four members of the 1982 World Cup squad in their team. They scored three goals that the goalie never saw.

SS: Having been lucky enough to go to Brazil, you got a sense of, 'Wow, we are part of something'. It was only when you saw what it meant to other people around the world that you really kind of thought about it. You came back and knew that this was something a little bit different to your regular non league club.

Chris Watney was also on the tour in 2001. His connection to the Casuals had started as a player in 1999 and he quickly became completely enamoured with the club and what it stood for. He studied the history, took it all in and fell head-over-heels in love. When he noted the hundredth anniversary of the aborted 1914 tour was approaching, he decided to try and arrange a trip to Brazil to mark that missed opportunity.

CW: I got taken to Brazil for the tour in 2001, and suddenly I was in the midst of this sort of Beatlemania type mayhem. I thought, 'Hang on, there's no chance I'm going to experience this at any other club'. I mean it's an absolutely unique experience and it just blew my mind. I just thought, 'I love this. I want to be more of a part of this.'

As 2014 approached, I thought it was only right that a hundred years on we try and go back and fulfil the matches that never happened - those games in 1914 that were cancelled - because the players only spent one day in Rio before going back straight away to fight in the war.

There were numerous snags in organising the tour, but Watney's commendable persistence paid off in the end. In 2015, a year later than planned, the Corinthian-Casuals arrived in São Paulo to a terrific welcome. The South London side was absolutely overwhelmed.

◀ *A programme from Corinthian-Casuals' 1988 visit to São Paulo Athletic Club, a club founded by English immigrants*

▲ *The Bandeira family, another group of Brazilian supporters, visit King George's Field*

CW: When we finally arrived I was so overjoyed. We came off the plane and were met with crowds at the airport – welcoming us, screaming and cheering, throwing Jamie Byatt up on their shoulders, all that sort of thing. It was an amazing moment to finally manage to get there.

Once again the non-leaguers were invited to play Corinthians Paulista, but there was a key difference this time – they weren't playing a veterans XI or the under-21s. For the first time in history, the first teams of Corinthians-Casuals and Corinthians Paulista played against one another, only eighteen months after Corinthians had been crowned FIFA World Club Champions with a victory over Chelsea.

CW: I think a couple of weeks beforehand we'd lost 4-0 to Folkestone, and now we're playing the world champions. We had Joe Hicks and Danny Dudley marking a striker called Paolo Guerrero who had just come back from winning the Golden Boot at the Copa América. You're thinking, 'God, what is going to happen here? This could be horrific!' But at half time it was still 0-0, and I'm told that the TV company didn't know what to do because they'd scheduled eight minutes of half-time just to replay the goals! So we'd really surprised everyone.

The noise was absolutely incredible. Playing in front of thirty thousand like that really got you excited and made you want to play. The pitch was so beautiful. The ball was so perfect. It felt like you couldn't really hit a bad pass, and there were passages where we actually played some quite nice football. In the pictures you can spot the occasional pink-and-brown shirt in the crowd. I think they would have gone mad if we'd scored.

It was amazing having that moment of the amateur on the pitch again with the professional. It harks right back to the day of playing professional teams as the amateur Corinthians.

In the end, the Brazilian superstars were able to make their quality show, winning 3-0 through second-half strikes - still a scoreline the Corinthian-Casuals could be enormously proud of. Then, in the spirit of Sócrates twenty-seven years earlier, a player from each side swapped shirts and Corinthian-Casuals legend Jamie Byatt became the first Englishman to play for Corinthians Paulista. He came agonisingly close to becoming their first English goalscorer too.

CW: The ball got nicked off his toe by a young Corinthians striker called Luciano who put it in. I'm told that the Corinthian players had a bit of a go at Luciano afterwards in the changing room because he'd stolen this great moment. It would have been a dream if Jamie had scored playing for Corinthians, but it's the ultimate pub quiz question: which English player played for the Brazilian champions in 2015? No one will know it, but Jamie did it.

There were other incredible touches, such as the Paulista side wearing on the back of their shirts the names of the original 1913 Corinthian FC players who lost their lives in the war. But while memories of the game itself are clearly special, many of the stories that Watney and his peers recall are those that concern the enduring fondness and raw emotion that Corinthians Paulista fans still reserve for their English counterparts, all those years after that first impression in 1910.

CW: We went to a children's cancer ward for a charity visit which was incredibly emotional. I think everyone was in tears when they left. We gave out shirts to the kids. We were told how much it was going to impact them and their families, just to break up their daily routine of trying to get better. Being in a position where you have the ability to actually affect people in that position was really humbling.

These kind of things caught everyone off guard - little things which you just don't think you have the ability to do when you're a non-league footballer in Tolworth.

One of the children to whom the players gave a Corinthian-Casuals shirt was a young boy who had been run over and developed cancer in his spine. The players signed his shirt, draped a scarf around his shoulders and posed for a photo with him, bringing a smile to his face. They could only wish him well and left the hospital deeply moved by his story.

A few days later they were told that the boy's pink-and-chocolate Casuals shirt had been auctioned off and had raised enough money to pay for the surgery he required. The players were astonished and emotions ran high when he visited their changing room, revealing that he could now even walk a little. In another story, Chris recalled working with a local fan group to raise over six tonnes of non-perishable food to be given to families in the favelas - they had asked for donations instead of a cover charge to watch the team train. In moments like these, the Casuals players realised the power of the shirt they wore week in, week out in the Isthmian League and what it meant to tens of thousands of people in Brazil.

Whether 1910, 1914, 1988, 2001, or 2015, there's no doubting the extraordinary nature of the story of the Brazilian tours, but considering the modest surroundings and unglamorous location of the present day Corinthian-Casuals, it's equally remarkable to consider those who make the reverse journey today. Countless Brazilian Corinthians fans feel the urge to make a pilgrimage to a small non-league ground in an unfashionable corner of the greater London area, simply because they see it as their club's spiritual home.

All share a burning passion to connect their present day support for Corinthians Paulista with the historical origins of their club, and they are often moved by the warm welcome they receive at King George's, with volunteers handing out free scarves and hats, or officials inviting them into the home dressing room to be photographed with members of the first team. Many cite Casuals superfan Roger Stringer as a particularly hospitable presence.

MARCO SIGNORI: I like the atmosphere, the mood, the supporters, Roger and everyone here. The first time I came here, these people helped me and treated me like a family member. It's priceless. Corinthians in Brazil are very well known for being a team that people would give blood for. The players, they play with love and I see exactly the same here.

RAFAEL FERREIRA: I come from São Paulo and have been a Corinthians fan since childhood. My father and my grandfather made me aware of the Corinthians-Casuals, and I always wanted to come here and see a match, so today is like a dream come true. It's like visiting the father of my club in Brazil.

ALBERT MONTE: In Brazil in 1910 soccer was only for rich people until the Corinthians came. Now, after a hundred and seven years, we have thirty-five million fans, and the Corinthian-Casuals are the beginning of this history, so it is very important for Corinthians fans to come here and visit.

I want to say thank you very much to Roger, who I first met at a game five years ago. I gave him a Corinthians banner and he's just told me that, for five years, at every Corinthian-Casuals match since, he has put it up. This gives me great pleasure.

Albert Monte has perhaps the best story of all the Brazilian characters that *Broadway to Brazil* met over the course of the 2017/18 season. It was a cold November afternoon, and the Casuals had just lost in the FA Trophy to Wingate & Finchley when Albert arrived at the ground with a suitcase trailing behind him.

AM: It has been a crazy day. I was supposed to arrive in London about one o'clock in the afternoon, two hours before kick off. One taxi and I should have had enough time before the game started.

But yesterday in São Paulo the rain delayed the flight by two hours. I arrived in Heathrow at three o'clock – I got through immigration, picked up my luggage, and then I came outside at four thirty. Then the taxi driver didn't know the address here! He goes

around and around. Afterwards I ask how much – '£100'. My God! £100 in Brazil you could have a big party and here I pay it for just one taxi. I arrived here one minute before the end of the game.

So I have a ticket for Tuesday night at Wembley stadium, Brazil against England. But maybe I'll change my plans because Corinthian-Casuals play on Tuesday also. I think I'll give my ticket to somebody else. I want to watch the Corinthian-Casuals game. It's more important than the Brazil game.

Albert stuck to his word. Should you happen to find yourself watching highlights from South Park v Corinthian-Casuals on Tuesday 14 November 2018, you can spot a particularly enthusiastic Albert celebrating goals scored by the Casuals, rushing forward to hug the players and generally looking like a man watching his team dominate a World Cup final. He had plenty to celebrate by the way – the Casuals ran out 6-1 winners that night, while England-Brazil finished a goalless draw. If Albert managed to recoup his Tolworth taxi fare through selling the ticket, you'd have to say he played an absolute blinder.

And so, at this juncture, *Broadway to Brazil* had reached the end of the road. Or so we thought. Having hung up the microphone, we found ourselves sucked back in just a year later, and this time we were going on a foreign trip of our own...

Listen to the full episode here:

SCAN ME

7 BROADWAY TO BUDAPEST

It's just gone 4pm on a hot and sticky summer's day in District 14. Two elderly sisters, aged eighty-eight and ninety-three, take their seats, having just arrived from northern Italy. They've travelled around six hundred miles to be here in Budapest, and they're here to take in a match between two amateur clubs from England and Hungary's lower levels of football.

Out on the pitch the touring Corinthian-Casuals players toil in the sweltering central European heat. For this assorted group of teachers, labourers and students, playing a match in 30-plus degrees is no normal thing. Then again, not much is normal about this particular occasion.

The match in question is the final of the Egri Erbstein Tournament, but why had two elderly women travelled from Italy to be here? What exactly is the Egri Erbstein Tournament? And what on earth were the Corinthian-Casuals doing in Budapest?

In the summer of 2018, just as the *Broadway to Brazil* series was wrapping up, writer and co-host of the show Dominic Bliss logged into his computer to find he had a mysterious email from a Hungarian stranger. This email was to kick off a chain of events that would culminate in the podcast team making a thousand-mile trip to watch Corinthian-Casuals in an international tournament.

◀ *The Corinthian-Casuals first team squad at the inaugural Egri Erbstein Tournament in Budapest, June 2019*

To explain how, we must start by calling in at the Austro-Hungarian Empire in 1916, where an eighteen year old midfielder named Ernő Egri Erbstein was about to make his debut for Budapesti Atlétikai Klub, or 'BAK' (pronounced 'bock' by the Hungarian tongue). Outside of *Broadway to Brazil*, Dominic Bliss is also the author of an influential biography of Erbstein, a Jewish-Hungarian genius described as football's forgotten pioneer. Providing the context of how the Casuals eventually ended up in Hungary a century later, Dominic began by revisiting Erbstein's eventful summer of 1916.

DOMINIC BLISS: He played for BAK for long stretches of his career, making his debut when he was eighteen in the middle of the First World War. That same summer he graduated from school with his equivalent of an 'A' Level, his maturity exam, which qualified him to be an army officer. So he enrolled in the Habsburg army and was sent to the front weeks after making his debut. I mean, that's a summer and a half! You graduate from school, pass your officers' exam, make your debut for a top flight football club, and then go to war.

After a modest playing career Erbstein made the move into coaching during the interwar years, achieving regional success at Italian clubs such as Bari, Cagliari and Nocerina. But it was when he pitched up at a tiny third division Tuscan side named AS Lucchese that the Hungarian really began to make waves. In a five-year spell he achieved two promotions and took the club to what is still their highest-ever league standing, seventh in Serie A. This success led to Erbstein being appointed to his most distinguished position, manager of Torino, and everywhere he went he introduced innovations that enabled his sides to punch well above their weight.

DB: He was one of the first in Italy to introduce pre-match warm-ups and dietary supplements. He imported vegetables from different parts of the country so that his players would have the best food available, things that most managers weren't thinking of until many years later. But he was also changing tactics and the way players look at the manager. He was like a cuddly uncle figure to them. He'd admonish them if they got out of hand but generally they saw him as someone that they could go to with their problems, and someone who would be able to speak to them on a human level as well as a sporting level. That's how he managed to eek more out of people than other managers, and it's why Torino employed him when they wanted to become a winning machine.

His players' love for him makes what happened next all the more tragic. As the 1930s progressed, Mussolini's Italy became an increasingly hostile place for its Jewish population. In 1938, just months after Erbstein had taken the Torino hotseat, laws were passed making Jews second class citizens, and he was forced to flee his adopted homeland and return to Hungary.

Wartime Budapest was no safe haven though. By 1944, fascists were in power in Hungary as well, and while Erbstein's wife and daughters found essential work in a factory, making military uniforms, he was forced to report to a labour camp. By way of a minor miracle, the whole family survived the unspeakable horrors of the Holocaust as Erbstein fled the camp shortly before they were due to be deported to Auschwitz, remarkably plotting a daring escape alongside future European Cup-winning coach, Béla Guttmann.

Despite those traumatic experiences, Erbstein never lost his passion for the beautiful game and his experiences of mankind's darkest hour only makes his postwar success all the more impressive. With the Italian political climate safe again, he returned to Turin and helped to build Il Grande Torino, a side who for many remain the greatest ever in Italian club history, winning five successive

Ernő Egri Erbstein in his ▶
Torino days

Serie A titles. His influence was felt far beyond the Italian peninsula.

DB: Hungary as a national team went from strength to strength off the back of what he and his coaching peers did, as did several Italian club sides. Barcelona became beneficiaries of these innovations because some of those Hungarian players signed for them. A lot of people trace Barcelona's modern day style to the Netherlands and Ajax total football sides of the 1970s. But they are connected in turn to Hungary of the 1950s, who themselves are connected to Erbstein's 1940s Torino. The thread of perfect football involves him but people lost his story.

Erbstein's life was cut short in 1949, along with his entire squad. As Il Grande Torino made their way home from a friendly in Portugal, their plane crashed into the basilica at the top of Superga hill that overlooks the city of Turin. All thirty-one passengers perished – including eighteen players and a fifty year old Ernő Egri Erbstein.

DB: The team killed in the air crash were the best players in the country and the backbone of the Italian national team – heroes at a time when postwar Italy sorely needed them. So the nation lost a dream team overnight, and I think the fact that this old Hungarian guy was the manager was almost a subplot, a secondary story. He was lost in the legacy of the great team that he managed.

Meanwhile in Hungary he was seen as a pre-communist figure – he had left the country before the Iron Curtain came down, and worked in the west. He was not someone the authorities wanted to place on a pedestal. Now if you're remembered neither in the country of your birth nor the country of your impact, you're not going to be remembered anywhere else either. So his name became completely forgotten.

▼ Erbstein with two of his Torino players on his way back from a friendly in Barcelona

▲ The newly reformed BAK team give the customary Hungarian pre-match salute

Completely forgotten, that is, until Dominic stumbled across it in an Italian football history book, dug a little deeper, and soon found himself penning *Erbstein: The triumph and tragedy of football's forgotten pioneer*, released in 2014.

One interested reader was Bertalan Molnár, a marketing director in Budapest's Zugló district where Erbstein's first club, BAK, used to play. When Bertalan picked up a copy of Dominic's book a few years after its release, he found that the more he learnt of the stories of Erbstein and BAK, the more he felt the hand of destiny on his shoulder.

BERTALAN MOLNÁR: I always say that the story found me – you know when something is just calling you to do something. BAK had vanished into the dark in 1947, and so I had the idea to re-establish this club that had existed here in the past. Then I found out about Egri Erbstein – how he had played for BAK for nine years and was a real icon of the team.

And so we renewed the club just over a year ago and it's been a dream journey. When you start of course it's a legal process – you sort have a frame but nothing else. But having a picture in the frame, that's a different story.

Bertalan took over the responsibilities of an existing club in the Hungarian sixth tier, changed their name to BAK and adopted the blue and black stripes that Erbstein had donned many a time. BAK were back. With his book having helped to inspire this rejuvenation, Dominic was made a club ambassador.

So, I hear you cry, what in God's name does any of this have to do with Tolworth's Corinthian-Casuals? Well, it all relates to the overseas travel by the Corinthian FC of yore, as we detailed in the previous chapter. We have briefly touched upon the Corinthian Cup, a gift from the English club, donated in 1905 to their Budapest brethren to

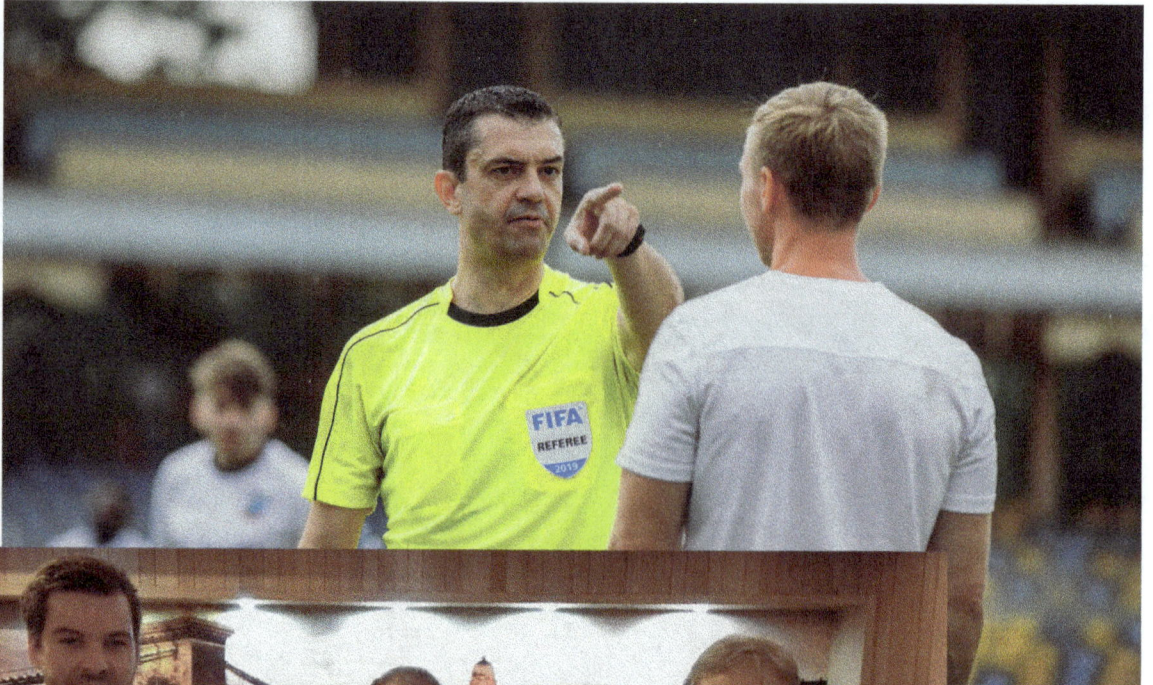

encourage amateur competition in Hungary. As it happens, it was the Corinthians who had the trophy minted, but it was the Casuals who handed it to their Hungarian friends a year later when they visited Budapest on their own European tour.

BAK were among the very first Corinthian Cup competitors and, when their new president discovered this wonderful piece of history, he had already started planning the creation of an international football tournament to be held in Egri Erbstein's name. Another piece of the jigsaw slotted into place when Dominic and Bertalan saw the opportunity to merge the two stories.

BM: I already knew Dominic had some involvement with the Corinthian-Casuals. Then I was at the computer when I discovered that BAK had played in the first-ever Corinthian Cup in Hungary. I just screamed in my study and my wife didn't know what had happened to me! I knew this was more than a coincidence, and it started the journey of Corinthian-Casuals becoming our sister club.

In the November of 2018, Dominic, Bertalan and Corinthian-Casuals director John Forrest met in a central Budapest restaurant and formalised the friendship between the two clubs. Over a bowl of goulash, they agreed to collaborate on the organisation of the inaugural Egri Erbstein Tournament to take place the following summer.

Fast forward eight months to an oppressively hot June day in Budapest and pink and brown flags, normally spotted in non league grounds in the south-east of England, are today tied to Hungarian wire fences. Familiar chants about Tolworth Tower are belted out by around 80 pitchside Londoners, who are basking not just in the sunshine but also the novelty of their side's European tour. The prospect of seeing Corinthian-Casuals lift some silverware was so compelling that not only have

◄ Top: *Champions League final referee, Viktor Kassai, at the Egri Ebstein Tournament* **Middle:** *Dominic Bliss, John Forrest, and Bertalan Molnár* **Bottom:** *Casuals pay tribute to Grande Torino team*

passports been dusted off, but some have been issued for the very first time. Among the crowd in the Szőnyi úti Stadion are individuals who have never left England before.

Groundsman and dedicated Casuals fan Dan Harris reflected on the novelty of the occasion.

DAN HARRIS: It's a bit different to Hythe away, this. It's thirty-five degrees here – I think it was about three degrees in Hythe! Taking loads of fans out here, playing in a tournament named after one of the most noble figures in football, is incredible. Here we are with a chance to win the first trophy for the club for a long time. No one could have imagined that this could happen to us a year or two ago. I'm not sure many teams at our level have done anything quite like this. It's absolutely mad really.

It was a uniquely Corinthian-Casuals experience, the latest in a series of eccentric club stories. As Dominic detailed, the twelve thousand capacity stadium added its own unique Soviet bloc charm to proceedings.

DB: The Szőnyi úti Stadion is brilliant. It's a crumbling concrete mid-20th century Soviet ground where you can see bits of reinforced steel coming through the steps where it's crumbled away. You have these kind of weird shaped pointy roofs over the main stand that don't really have architectural twins anywhere in the world and I don't know what I would call them - they're like IKEA turrets or something. A yellow and blue triangular roof. But it also has a gantry, a VIP area, bucket seats, standing terracing, and a bar. Everything we need to make a tournament. Perfect.

The stadium, of course, was among the many logistics that Bertalan, Dominic and the organising team had to tackle. They also needed to invite two other sides, with historic local amateur clubs BEAC and Testvériség agreeing to compete. Trophies had to be created, and a new spectacular Corinthian Cup was minted, along with smaller prizes for the other competitors.

▲ BAK's unexpected new supporters, Duran Duran

They had to find tournament officials too, and they didn't do too badly on this front, with 2011 Champions League final referee and native Hungarian Viktor Kassai recruited as the man in the middle. Then a buzz had to be generated, which it was, through the 'i' newspaper and BBC London Radio, among others. A bit of star power didn't hurt on this front: Petr Cech shared the story to his millions of Twitter followers, while the Casuals also received a goodwill video message from a fellow Corinthian, Brazil international David Luiz.

Then there was the question of getting the Casuals over to Hungary. A GoFundMe campaign was stunning in its success, raising £5000 in a matter of weeks, before being bolstered by an extraordinary individual donation from former Casuals player John Balson that tipped the fundraising total over its target. As the tournament edged closer

and closer to becoming a reality, Dominic was increasingly impressed by the organisational skills of his friends from Hungary, which extended to correspondence with 1980s New Wave pop stars.

DB: There was a little bit of a buzz starting to generate, and I'm thinking how ramshackle this is going to be because I'm at the centre of it and it's terrifying. But I didn't realise how all the people involved in running BAK over in Budapest were not ramshackle at all. They had everything sorted. They had arranged everything.

They had even got Duran Duran to give us permission to use My Own Way as the official tournament song. Bertalan told me he wanted to do this and my reaction was, 'They're not going say yes, they're just going to ignore your email'. Well, I ate humble pie. They didn't just come back saying, 'Yes, please do use our song, you've got our permission'. They also said, 'We love the story behind your club, can you send us shirts please?' So Bertalan sent them personalised shirts, which they then posed with and posted across their social media channels. There were thousands and thousands of shares, which is ridiculous for an amateur club. So Bertalan was right; I was wrong. It was a great idea. It gained us news coverage in several countries and four extremely famous supporters.

Now it was time for the tangible realisation of all this planning. The Egri Erbstein Tournament consisted of four teams contesting two semi finals, followed by a third-place play-off and a final. Saturday's second semi-final would see student side BEAC take on former state railway club Testvériség, but the main event and curtain raiser for the competition was the chocolate and pink of Corinthian-Casuals taking on the black and blue of BAK.

Opposite the roofless stand where some of the Casuals hardcore were slowly frying in the open air, *Broadway to Brazil* spoke to a few intrigued locals: Áron Aranyossy, a sports journalist in Budapest, and Kevin McClusky, a Budapest-based Scotsman who had started following BAK after discovering their story online.

ÁRON ARANYOSSY: I honestly expect the Corinthian-Casuals to walk this tournament to be honest. But who knows? As long as BAK keep their structure and positioning, and remain very calm and organised, they might make this interesting. I don't think it will be a crazy goal parade, but I do believe that Casuals should have this match in their pocket.

KEVIN MCCLUSKY: I actually think as the game goes on BAK will become the stronger team because of the heat. Casuals have a more physical side than BAK but I think the heat will play a part as the game goes on. We're heading to thirty-four, thirty-five degrees and us Brits aren't used to that!

▼ *Corinthian-Casuals and BAK join for a photo after their semi-final*

It's certainly true that, despite the Casuals being strong favourites, BAK did not roll over. A spirited performance saw them hold their English hosts to a half-time stalemate, but quality saw through in the end, as a trio of second half strikes ensured the game finished 3-0 to the touring side.

It was comfortable enough, but not the cricket score that some had speculated, and hosts BAK left the pitch with their heads held high. The Casuals players meanwhile were just happy to survive the heat, as captain and goalkeeper Danny Bracken relaid.

DANNY BRACKEN: It's a lot different to a Tuesday night at Ramsgate. It's something that you'll only ever experience if you come and play in the European summer like this, but I thought we adapted to it okay, although the tempo in the first half was too slow. They have players who can pass the ball, who technically are quite good, but what they lacked was a little bit of physicality and a little bit of mobility, so as soon as we got close to them we were able to get the ball back a little easier.

This will be my ninth year at the Casuals, and I've never won anything so it would be nice to lift the trophy. We know it's going to be hard and the conditions might be against us, although hopefully there'll be a little more cloud tomorrow and the temperatures will drop a little bit. I want to win, and my brother wants to win his first trophy as the Casuals manager as well.

The day's other semi-final was less tight, and the several levels that separated Testvériség from student side BEAC were obvious as the former ran out 8-0 winners. As widely expected, the first Egri Erbstein Tournament final would be Corinthian-Casuals vs the team known locally as 'Tesi'.

Sunday's action took place in slightly cooler conditions after forecasted thunderstorms came to pass. Prior to the final, the bronze medal match between BEAC and BAK went the way of Bertalan's team, who turned around a 1-0 deficit late in the game to win 2-1. As the Testvériség and Corinthian-

Casuals teams came out for the main event, Dan Harris gave *Broadway to Brazil* a brief insight into the opposition based on yesterday's eight-goal semi-final performance.

DH: I saw them play yesterday and they looked quite decent, and their keeper dives around like Stretch Armstrong! It will be a good test for us. It's not as hot as yesterday, and we've had a bit of rain, so that helps. I think we should know in the first ten minutes how it's going to go. I don't really know what's going to happen to be honest.

The match largely followed the blueprint of the semi-final, with the Casuals struggling to break down an organised opposition content to play on the counter. Unlike BAK, Tesi's defensive wall refused to buckle, and their goalkeeper blocked just about everything thrown his way. Dan's Stretch Armstrong scouting report was right on the money!

With the clock racing towards ninety minutes, it dawned on everyone of a Casuals persuasion that this was becoming a carbon copy of the club's last two final appearances - a strong display, a hatful of chances, and a total inability to get any of them past a superhuman keeper. Without a goal in the dying minutes, this final was headed to the exact same conclusion as those play-offs back in England: penalties. And nobody would fancy this keeper to let many in.

Manager James Bracken believed he had the tools at his disposal to make that goal happen, bringing winger Emil Salama and striker Harry Ottaway off the bench. *Broadway to Brazil* host Jarek Zaba stood with club director John Forrest and clubhouse manager Martin Foley for the closing stages, all three increasingly losing their composure as chance after chance went begging. But, emulating the joyous chaos that greeted the injury time equaliser at Hythe as covered in Episode 5, Jarek once again was able to capture the moment of raw unbridled jubilation for our podcast special.

Celebrations in Budapest ▶

Believe it or not, it was the same man who made it happen. Bracken's double sub paid dividends as Salama and Ottaway combined in the 91st minute to provide the striker with a two-yard open goal tap-in, and he made no mistake.

The match finished 1-0 to Corinthian-Casuals, and they were the first ever champions of the Egri Erbstein Tournament. As the players made their way to the covered stand for the trophy presentations, the fans who had spent the last two days under the beating sun – now slightly redder in complexion – followed suit. The whole Corinthian-Casuals contingent joined as one as Danny Bracken hoisted the brand new Corinthian Cup into the air.

DBr: You don't get this at any other club. We're very very lucky to play for Corinthian-Casuals and have experiences like this. I might be earning a few quid at another club but these experiences are once in a lifetime, and we're very lucky to have them. You can't buy memories.

Supporters were no less enthused. For those more used to Bognor than Budapest, those who had shed tears at play-off final defeats in years gone by, this was a special moment.

JOHN FORREST: Incredible. Just incredible. I'm lost for words.

JACK SMITH: Absolutely unreal. I can't put it into words really, I'm still trying to get over it. All of us out here in Budapest, and we've just watched Casuals win the cup with a 90th minute winner. I've kissed the cup, I've lifted the cup! It's just surreal mate, absolutely surreal.

It's special, because although it's officially a friendly tournament, it's in honour of a great man in football history that many people have forgotten about. Like everyone, I didn't have a clue until this

▼ *Travelling Corinthian-Casuals fans celebrate being 'champions of Europe'*

▲ Dominic Bliss is joined by Susanna and Marta Egri, the daughters of Egri Erbstein, at the final

tournament. Now I've read up on the guy, it's actually insane how much he helped to make football what it is today. And we're Corinthian-Casuals, we've helped shape football around the world. So the way it has come together is just brilliant.

When *Broadway to Brazil* caught up with James Bracken, he and his squad were on their way to an end-of-tournament dinner with all the other competitors, a fine symbol of the bonds of brotherhood that were established in the name of Egri Erbstein.

JAMES BRACKEN: It's been great. Full on but great. Yesterday we played in boiling hot heat – too hot to sit in, never mind run around and play ninety minutes off the back of no pre-season. But credit to the lads, they got through it and got the result we needed to put ourselves in this position today, and then we've finished the job off fantastically well.

Everyone in the squad has done well. I can't speak highly enough of all of them. I've got two players, Kevat Serbonij and Jack Tucker, who have played two full ninety minutes in two days. Jesus, I'm knackered just standing there! And they've worked their absolute socks off for the club like they always do. It's a thoroughly deserved victory for us.

I think there's a hundred of us going out for a nice meal now which is great. We are a club with a fantastic history, more history than most, but we make sure that the players are aware that they have to come and represent the club in a certain way. We're certainly winners as we've proved here and we continue to prove back home – we're no one's mugs. But at the same time we know how to behave, we know how to conduct ourselves, we know how to be gracious in victory and defeat. The boys have done everything that I could have asked.

Of course the tournament was much more than just a trophy for the chocolate and pink. The two elderly women in attendance described at the start of this chapter were Susanna and Marta Egri, the daughters of Ernő Egri Erbstein. They came to the tournament to honour their father's legacy, alongside Marta's son, Stefano. He spoke to *Broadway to Brazil* about the symbolic importance of the occasion, in particular pointing to the influence of the English game on his grandfather's philosophy.

STEFANO EGRI: It has been a great event and we are very grateful to Corinthians-Casuals. It was an English style of football that my grandfather introduced to European countries. He had a very English philosophy, especially when it came to fair play which I think is at the heart of amateur football. So it means a lot to have an English team here to celebrate his legacy after so many years, the first we have had since he passed away.

Another guest of honour at the final was Antonio Comi, the sporting director of Torino FC, who was particularly touched to see the Casuals team take to the pitch in commemorative shirts, each displaying the name of a player from Erbstein's tragic Grande Torino side.

The ultimate vision for the Egri Erbstein Tournament organisers is to establish a well-known regular international competition for non-league club sides, with the next hurdle being the need for sponsorship so that more sides can afford to travel abroad and compete with like-minded opposition. To see the Casuals fans singing the names of their Hungarian opponents and vice versa, the spirit of fair play, camaraderie and sportsmanship was positively pumping through this tournament's veins.

Ultimately, Dominic was able to reflect on a weekend in which the seemingly separate histories of Erbstein and the Casuals came together and shared a bond.

◄ *Captain Danny Bracken with the newly minted Corinthian Cup*

DB: I like to reflect on all those moments where people from very different backgrounds were enjoying themselves. I think of Dan Harris, a groundsman at Casuals thanking me for organising the tournament because he's had such a brilliant time. I think about people like Billy, Jack and the other fans, going mad celebrating the win. Then I think about the Egris, Marta and Susanna, understanding and appreciating what we were doing in their dad's name.

I broke down in tears when the BAK and Corinthian-Casuals players came over to the stand at the end of the game to acknowledge the fans. They posed for a joint team photo, and the Casuals fans started singing one of the club anthems, which moved me. Then they immediately followed it up by singing the name of BAK, and the players joined in. That was really quite something.

I think the tournament perfectly reflected what binds the Erbstein and the Corinthian stories. It's not immediately obvious but Erbstein believed in playing with a smile, playing the right way, motivating people with an arm around the shoulder. In very simple terms he was a Corinthian. His phrase was play fair, smile and pass the ball, and that's what everyone did that weekend. It was the perfect way to honour the two stories behind the Egri Erbstein Tournament for the Corinthian Cup.

Listen to the full episode here:

SCAN ME

ACKNOWLEDGEMENTS

The *Broadway to Brazil* production team met for the first time at a pre-season match between Corinthian-Casuals and Bristol Rovers on a sunny evening at King George's Field. We stood in the section of terracing to the left of the directors' box in the main stand that has since become known as the home of the Torcida Seething and watched as our local Isthmian League South team defeated League One opposition with a fine display of attacking football.

We left impressed by the players and the coaching team that had put together such a promising side from local amateur footballers, but also imbued with a sense of possibility. It was immediately clear to us that the club was a source of infinite stories and the people at Corinthian-Casuals would soon become our friends.

Shortly afterwards we began to meet regularly at The Lamb in Surbiton, to catch up and discuss the shape our podcast series would take. We came up with the name *Broadway to Brazil* in our first meeting and soon we were apportioning the workload and dividing the narrative into episodes. It came together naturally, but not without the hard work and commitment of everyone involved, and as we move this story from podcast to page, a new aspect has opened up to us. Stuart Tree's photography is as central to the telling of these events as any of our words, and his hard work and devotion in running the club's media channels for many years has left all of us awed.

However, as well as the core podcast team – Jarek, Dominic, Tony, John and Brent – there were many other people whose help and support were crucial to the creation of the podcast and, now, this book.

Robin Hutchinson, a totemic figure of several community projects in Kingston-upon-Thames and the surrounding area, was there at the beginning of it all. He introduced us to one another, got us together in one place, and let the magic flow. Ann Hutchinson was full of ideas and suggestions throughout the project and her cries of 'Reeeeallly!?' at questionable refereeing decisions over the course of our time following the club have become the stuff of legend.

Without the members of the Torcida Seething and the staff at The Lamb, all of whom put up with our terrible terrace chants and noisy podcast discussions, we would not have enjoyed this journey half as much. We also owe a debt of gratitude to Kelly Bliss, who designed our artwork, and Chris Kelly, who created and managed our website.

We are eternally grateful to the supporters and volunteers at Corinthian-Casuals who made us feel welcome from the start, and to James Bracken and his players for being such a key part of the podcast. We thank Brian Vandervilt and the committee for all their help and support, as well as Micky and Alec Stewart, the Phillips brothers, Chris Watney, Martin Tyler, and all the interviewees who gave up their time to share their stories. We also wish to thank the good people at BAK, for their wonderful hospitality in Budapest. We will see you all again!

Finally, this book owes a huge amount to the millions of Corinthians fans in Brazil and around the world whose passion inspired this story.

Vai Corinthians!

Website: broadwaytobrazil.com
Twitter: @broadway2brazil
Facebook: @BroadwayToBrazil

ABOUT THE COMMUNITY BRAIN

The Community Brain was founded over ten years ago with the belief that everyone is brilliant if they are given the support to be brilliant. We work to encourage community cohesion using the widest range of the arts, education and local history in order to give people and place renewed importance and pride. We want to help release people's natural talents and energies to develop stronger communities and relationships.

At the heart of all of our work are stories. Who tells the story of your life? How can we create the stories that celebrate our communities? How do you re-imagine and curate your own future story?

We also have a never-ending passion for laughter and play. Many of our community projects start in a place of discovery through smiling, feeling like you are back in the playground, learning about ourselves and others through enjoying our lives and the time and space we share.

We believe in Generosity. We believe in Creativity. We believe in Curiosity. We believe in Adventure.

The work we do with communities involves no formal joining or membership. This is not about clubs or cliques. All we strive for is giving people the permission they don't really need to be as brilliant as they already can be. In this way we're told we have helped change the lives of people who may not have found the usual and 'ordinary' routes to engaging in their community suitable for them. They have begun to command their own story instead of following the one written for them by others.

You can find out more and how to get involved at thecommunitybrain.org

Jarek Zaba

Stuart Tree

Dominic Bliss

Tony Banks

John Forrest

Brent Davies

Santhini Koshy

Jocelyn Pontes

Klara Armstrong

Alexane Rondolat

Robin Hutchinson

MEET THE TEAM

Jarek Zaba

Jarek is a writer and audio production specialist. Since graduating from Kingston University in 2009, he has worked as an oral historian on a number of local heritage projects. *Broadway to Brazil* crystallised a passion for audio that led him to complete an MA in Radio at Goldsmiths. Originally hailing from the West Midlands, Jarek can be found supporting Aston Villa when not at the Casuals.

Dominic Bliss

Dominic is a London-based sports journalist, who has made his name as an interviewer and writer of sports profile pieces. He is currently the features editor of the Chelsea FC publications and has travelled the continent covering football at the highest level. His first book, *Erbstein: The triumph and tragedy of football's forgotten pioneer*, is a biography of the Grande Torino coach and Holocaust survivor, Ernő Egri Erbstein.

Tony Banks

Tony has been a football reporter with the *Daily Express* for 20 years. He covers Premier League football for his work, but his love of non-league football has never gone away. In his early days, he covered games in the Kingston area for local papers, with teams such as Kingstonian, Hampton & Richmond and Hounslow. He would have covered Casuals had they not been playing in Tooting or Molesey at the time!

Brent Davies

Brent was producer and co-editor on the *Broadway to Brazil* podcast. He also produced a sponsored live 24-hour podcast, raising money for a local charity. He is a lifelong Millwall fan and follower of non-league football. Being involved with the podcast and living close to the ground lead to a close affinity with the club, and the Casuals gained another supporter as a result.

John Forrest

John is a Committee Member at Corinthian-Casuals FC where he volunteers as the Community Officer as well as running the club shop. A self-confessed vexillologist, he can typically be found hanging a startling number of flags at King George's Field on matchdays. John originally hails from Dewsbury in West Yorkshire and is a recovering Huddersfield Town supporter.

Stuart Tree

Stuart has been the Corinthian-Casuals' official photographer for nearly a decade, photographing over four hundred matches. His photography has taken him as far as Hungary and Brazil, where he was the club's tour snapper. Outside of photography, Stuart is also an award-winning programme editor, having won multiple accolades for his Casuals matchday programme over the years.

Robin Hutchinson

Robin has something wrong with his brain, still believing anything is possible. He is a Director of The Community Brain, a CIC established to help support, energise, develop and nurture communities. They opened the Museum of Futures in Surbiton and subsequently fitted the Community Kitchen. They run SHEDx 'Growing Ideas in Tolworth'. It is through this work that Robin developed his interest in Corinthian-Casuals and their amazing story.

Klara Armstrong
Project Leader & Editorial

Klara is a Creative Writing graduate and Kingston MA Publishing student whose writing retains a strong mental health focus. She never leaves home without a notebook and something to read, even whilst travelling around the country (and occasionally across Europe) to watch Chelsea FC. Currently, Klara is working on her debut poetry collection and novel.

Santhini Koshy
Cover & Interior Design

Santhini is an experienced copywriter with a flair for design who has developed an interest in the book business. In her free time she also likes to play the guitar and write copious amounts of poetry. She is still adjusting to the British weather and eagerly awaits her first trip to Anfield.

Jocelyn Pontes
Cover & Interior Design

Jocelyn is a Creative Writing & Publishing MA student at Kingston University London. She holds a BFA degree in Writing, Literature & Publishing from Emerson College in Boston, Massachusetts. She is working toward a career in publishing, with a focus on the design and editorial aspects of the business. She also enjoys writing fiction and aims to become a published author.

Alexane Rondolat
Editorial

Alexane is a Publishing MA student at Kingston University with a Publishing Media Bachelor's degree from Oxford Brookes University. After her studies, she aims to work in the publishing industry either in the editorial or in the foreign rights department.

About Kingston University Press

Kingston University Press has been publishing high-quality commercial and academic titles for over ten years. Our list has always reflected the diverse nature of the student and academic bodies at the university in ways that are designed to impact on debate, to hear new voices, to generate mutual understanding and to complement the values to which the university is committed.

Increasingly the books we publish are produced by students on the MA Publishing and BA Publishing courses, often working with partner organisations to bring projects to life. While keeping true to our original mission, and maintaining our wide-ranging backlist titles, our most recent publishing focuses on bringing to the fore voices that reflect and appeal to our community at the university as well as the wider reading community of readers and writers in the UK and beyond.

This book was edited, designed, typeset and produced by students on the MA Publishing course at Kingston University, London.

To find out more about our hands-on, professionally focused and flexible MA and BA programmes please visit:

www.kingston.ac.uk
www.kingstonpublishing.wordpress.com
@kingstonjourno
@KU_press